DISCOVERY WALKS
in
CARMARTHENSHIRE

John Fenna

Copyright © J. Fenna, 1998

Published by Sigma Leisure – an imprint of
Sigma Press, 1 South Oak Lane, Wilmslow, Cheshire SK9 6AR, England.

British Library Cataloguing in Publication Data
A CIP record for this book is available from the British Library.

ISBN: 1-85058-633-0

Typesetting and Design by: Sigma Press, Wilmslow, Cheshire.

Cover photograph: Looking down the track from Hafod to Ty Lllwyd near Brechfa.

Maps: Alan Bradley

Printed by: MFP Design and Print

Preface

I hope that this collection of walks leads to visitors and locals enjoying the superb scenery of Carmarthenshire from the healthiest, cheapest and – to me at least – the most pleasurable method of transport – walking on your own two feet.

I would like to thank everyone who helped me in producing this book especially the following: The Ordnance Survey – especially Steven Yates – without whose maps the walks could not have been attempted; Sue Parrot, Brecon Beacons National Park Head Warden; Mr G.D. Williams, the Area Secretary, Dyfed Area of The Ramblers' Association; Philip James, National Trust Area Manager; and Mike Scott, of Forest Enterprise, who all checked that the routes described were not going to cause any problems and corrected small errors in the draft of this book as well as giving additional information. Thanks also to Hazel Jones for reading (and correcting) the typescript and proofs, and to Ruth, Pauline, Raph and Garry for walking some of the routes with me to check that my descriptions of the walks were comprehensible.

Last, but far from least, my wife Lis, who has not only typed most of this work but also runs the household as well as holding down a full-time job!

John Fenna

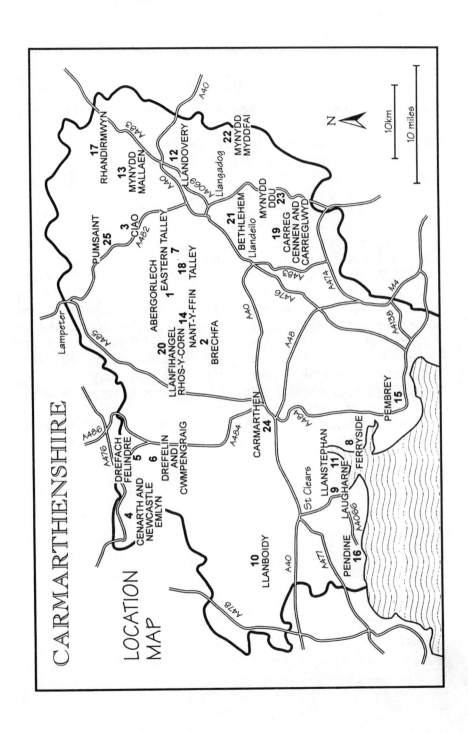

CARMARTHENSHIRE

LOCATION MAP

N

10km
10 miles

1 EASTERN TALLEY
2 BRECHFA
3 CIAO
4 CENARTH AND NEWCASTLE EMLYN
5 DREFACH FELINDRE
6 DREFELIN AND CWMPENGRAIG
7 TALLEY
8 FERRYSIDE
9 PENDINE
10 LLANBOIDY
11 LAUGHARNE
12 LLANDOVERY
13 MYNYDD MALLAEN
14 NANT-Y-FFIN
15 PEMBREY
16 PENDINE
17 RHANDIRMWYN
18 ABERGORLECH
19 CARREG CENNEN AND CARREGLWYD
20 LLANFIHANGEL RHOS-Y-CORN
21 BETHLEHEM
22 MYNYDD MYDDFAI
23 MYNYDD DDU
24 CARMARTHEN
25 PUMSAINT

Lampeter
Llangadog
Llandeilo
St Clears
Llanstephan

A40, A482, A485, A476, A484, A48, A40, A477, A478, A4069, A483, A474, A476, A4138, M4, A4066, A464

Contents

Introduction

The Carmarthenshire countryside and coastline offers a variety of scenery from sand dunes and towering sea cliffs to moorland and crags, from rolling farmland and deep wooded valleys to river gorges and tidal marshes. All of these various landscapes offer superb walking and the choice of different types of scenery in a small area.

Man has left his mark on the landscape in a variety of ways, with prehistoric features such as cairns, cromlechs and hill forts, standing stones and hut circles being found in abundance. More recent signs of man's influence on the area are Roman, Celtic and Norman remains, as well as disused quarries, old railway lines and old 'green roads', while the rural landscape has been totally formed by changing farm practices.

Carmarthenshire is famous for its wealth of wild flowers and plants, some of them rare. The wide variety of growing conditions means a wide variety of species, and at most times of the year you can find many of these in flower. Spring is a riot of colour, and in autumn the hills are ablaze with the combined glory of gorse and heather.

This wide range of habitats also gives a great diversity to the bird life. The coast is naturally a haven for a wide variety of seabirds, while various birds of prey, notably the buzzard, but also kestrels, peregrines, kites and others, will be seen (with the buzzards often seen) patrolling the hills.

Mammals are also seen in great variety, from dolphins and seals in the bays, where seal pups are a charming addition to the rocky coves when newborn and nearly helpless, to signs of badgers and foxes in most parts. On the hills you will find many roaming ponies and sheep, while Welsh Black cattle will be found on many farms.

When out walking, I would recommend you carry good field guides to bird, mammal and plant life (Collins Gem Books are excellent), and a pair of binoculars to help identify the wildlife and flowers.

The appropriate OS maps are listed for each walk and as well as helping you find your way, these fascinating documents can tell you much about the area in which the walk is set. At the time of writing, the OS are in the process of replacing the Pathfinder 1 to 25 000 scale maps with the new Explorer 1 to 25 000 scale maps. Explorer maps 10 (164), 177, 178, 185, 186, 187B and 198A, along with Outdoor Leisure 12 (Brecon Beacons National Park Western Area) should give you complete coverage of Carmarthenshire. I cannot yet say, however, which walks will definitely fall onto which maps (in most cases) since, as I write, the maps are not yet published.

I strongly advise that at any time of year walkers carry a full set of waterproofs, some extra food and warm clothing, a small first aid kit and a survival bag, as a minimum in case of emergency. As a matter of course, carrying a map and compass, and the knowledge of how to use them, will help prevent getting mislaid (never lost), while good walking boots or stout shoes are highly recommended for all walking.

To cater for walkers who use miles and those who use kilometres, I have used both types of measurements in this book.

Rights and Responsibilities

I have done my best to ensure that all the walks are on public paths and rights of way, or are at least with the landowner's permission. Please try to keep to the route described and follow the Country Code at all times. It should be noted that at times the route described does not exactly follow the paths shown on the excellent Ordnance Survey maps. This can be explained by various factors including 'common usage' and locally agreed diversions, permissive paths and, in open country, agreed access. Errors on the maps are rare. Occasionally paths will change, and if a new diversion is in place the route may be diverted from that shown on the map or described in the text.

Remember that some paths will have other user rights – on bridleways you can expect to meet horses and cyclists as well as other walkers, while you may also meet vehicles on some of the 'green lanes'.

Treat it as a privilege to be able to walk across someone else's land and an atmosphere of co-operation, not confrontation, can be forged. However, should you have any problem in following any of the routes due to unreasonable diversion or obstruction of a right of way, send full details (including grid references) to the Welsh Officer of the Ramblers' Association, Ty'r Cerddwyr, High Street, Gresford, Wrexham, LL12 8PT (Telephone 01978 855148).

Many of the walks follow paths close to natural and man-made hazards, cliff edges and river banks, farm works, quarries etc., where appropriate care is necessary, especially if you have children with you.

The Country Code

❖ Guard against all risk of fire.

❖ Fasten all gates.

❖ Keep dogs under proper control.

❖ Avoid damaging fences, hedges and walls.

❖ Keep to paths across farmland.

❖ Leave no litter.

❖ Safeguard water supplies.

❖ Protect water supplies.

❖ Protect wildlife, wild plants and trees.

❖ Go carefully on country roads.

❖ Respect the life of the countryside.

Seals

Please note and follow the advice in this extract from the Dyfed Wildlife Trust's 'The Grey Seal Code of Conduct'.

If you come across a seal on the beach:

❖ Withdraw immediately and leave it alone.

❖ Do not fuss around the pup – the mother will probably be watching anxiously from the safety of the waves, and may abandon the pup if humans are in the vicinity.

❖ Do not let other people disturb the pup.

❖ Keep dogs well away.

❖ Do not move or handle the pup, drive it off the beach, try to get it into the sea, feed it or try to take it home (seals can give a very nasty bite).

If you think the pup has been abandoned:

❖ Retire and observe from a distance (preferably down-wind) to see if the mother returns, and keep others from disturbing the pup. If the mother does not return within four hours, call the RSPCA/Dyfed Wildlife Trust Seal Network.

If the pup is obviously sick or injured:

❖ Call the RSPCA/Dyfed Wildlife Trust Seal Network immediately on 01990 555999, do not try to move it or care for it yourself. If you find a dead seal, do not handle it as it may carry infectious diseases. Call the Strandings Line immediately on 01348 875000.

Forestry Code

❖ Guard against all risks of fire.

❖ Protect trees, plants and wildlife.

❖ Leave things as you find them, take nothing away.

❖ Keep dogs and animals under proper control.

❖ Avoid damaging buildings, fences, hedges, walls and signs.

❖ Leave no litter, respect the work of the forest.

❖ Observe all signs, do not leave open or obstruct gates.

❖ For your own safety, keep clear of forestry operations.

❖ Respect the peace and quiet of the forest and avoid disturbing others.

Remember: Take only photographs – leave only footprints.

1: Abergorlech Forest

Distance: 8½ miles (13.75 km)

Time: 4 hours

Maps: OS Landranger 146 Lampeter and Llandovery, OS Pathfinder 1035 Pencader

Start: Picnic site, Abergorlech 586 337

Terrain: Mainly well-graded forestry tracks. Two awkward fords and one steep, narrow path downhill. Some muddy sections.

Nearest Towns: Lampeter, Llandovery, Carmarthen.

Parking: See Start

Refreshments: Post office and shop and the excellent Black Lion pub in Abergorlech.

Stiles: None

Suitable for: All the family.

Along the way

This walk takes you through the eastern part of the famous Brechfa Forest, which, although now managed by Forestry Enterprise, part of the Forestry Commission, for both timber production and recreation, has a long history.

In the Middle Ages the forest was mainly of oak and ash trees and was an important hunting ground, indeed a Royal Hunting Forest. Until the early 20th century wood from the forest was harvested to fuel the industrial needs of South Wales. As well as playing its part in the Industrial Revolution, in the First World War timber from the forest was taken to produce naphtha for use in making explosives!

In 1919 the Forestry Commission was created to re-establish the depleted forests of Britain, and it was then that much of the conifer plantation work in the forest was done. Much work was experimental and many species were tried, providing some diversity. In these days of 'multi-purpose forestry', recreation and wildlife conservation play a greater role than has previously been the case, and are just as important as timber production in the work of Forest Enterprise.

Luckily, many parts of the 'ancient woodland' still survive in Brechfa Forest and as well as great stands of conifers, you will find extensive areas of hardwood trees such as aspen, oak, ash, rowan, hazel, hawthorn (and I am sure I saw a eucalyptus!) and wild flowers abound. This provides a wider variety of wildlife than you might expect from many Forest Enterprise woods, with many song birds as well as buzzards, red kites and goshawks being seen in the air. On the ground you may find traces of many mammals from the smaller rodents up to foxes. An exciting sighting would be the rare pine marten, which I understand has a toe-hold in the area.

The village of Abergorlech enjoys a fine situation by the confluence of the Gorlech and Cothi rivers, and boasts an attractive church, an excellent pub (with extensive menu) and a fine bridge of probable 16th-century origin.

The bridge at Abergorlech

The intriguing 'Gorlech Stones' seen decorating the gardens and houses in the village were once thought to be fossilized animals, but are actually nodules of iron-rich mudstone which became cracked when drying. The cracks filled with calcite, a much harder mineral, which resisted erosion, while the soft mudstone wore away. This has resulted in the interesting forms now displayed in these local curiosities.

Note that there are many more tracks than are marked on the OS maps, while some shown on the maps do not exist on the ground!

The Route

From the picnic site, take the broad track through the iron gate at the back of the site, up the side of the River Gorlech. Follow this major track for some 900 metres through mixed broadleaved and coniferous woods, with the rushing stream below on your left, up to a track junction under a crag of shale.

1. Turn right up the track, following a white 'permitted footpath' waymark. Climb gently up, initially through mainly oak woods with crags on your left, and a small stream noisily obvious but hidden in a deep cleft on your right.

2. Follow this track up the Nant Llywelau-bach for approximately 1500 metres, ignoring any tracks coming in from the right, until you come to a crossroads of tracks. Turn left, again following the white waymarks, and almost double back above the track you have just come up.

   As the track loops around Banc Llywelau, extensive views open up on your left that include the Brecon Beacons, the Gorlech and Cothi Valleys and the hills in between. This section of the walk clearly illustrates the job of the foresters, with the patchwork of various plantings and harvestings, as well as a cycle route and path waymarking clearly visible.

3. Follow the major track for one and a half miles from the crossroads of tracks at the head of Nant Llywelau-bach to a fork in the track, where one branch descends left and one climbs right. Take nei-

ther but drop sharp left by a white waymark post, almost doubling back on yourself as you zigzag down a steep, narrow footpath through the trees, down to a broad track in the bottom of the Gorlech valley.

4. Turn right, then almost immediately take the left fork as the track divides. Stay on the major track for approximately one and a half miles until you come to a fork in the track by Trawscoed, a house on the edge of the woods. Take the left fork past the back of the house, then go left at a crossroads of tracks, once again almost doubling back on yourself.

   Follow the track for approximately 200 metres to where a narrow, rutted footpath drops left down to the junction of two streams. Follow the footpath to the water and then, perhaps with some difficulty, cross to the far, south-western bank. In summer this should not be difficult to manage dry-shod, but in wet weather may prove impossible until the proposed bridge is installed. If you cannot cross, return to the track, turn left and follow it on a detour of a little more than one and a half miles around the head of the stream, rejoining the described route further on.

5. If you do manage to cross the stream, you find an ideal spot for a brief rest (perhaps to dry out socks). A clear bridleway runs from the stream crossing up to the forestry track. On reaching this track, turn left and follow it, the main forestry track, down the western side of the Gorlech valley for about one and three-quarters of a mile. This is the track those diverting around the stream crossing will come on, down from higher up the valley.

6. After passing through a deep cutting you come to a T-junction of tracks. Turn left and zigzag down to a bridge across the river and another T-junction of tracks. Turn right and follow this track, now with the river on your right, for some 300 metres to where a narrower track joins from the right.

7. Take this track back down to a ford across the river. This ford can be difficult in high water conditions when I would suggest you simply follow the main track down the eastern side of the river back to the start. However, it is usually possible to cross dry-shod (gaiters

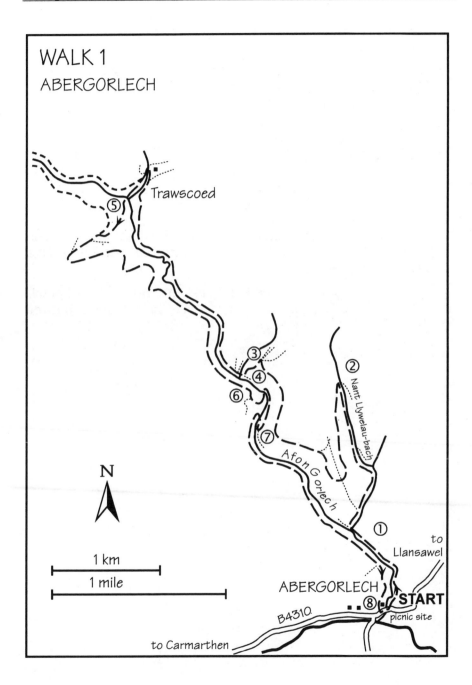

WALK 1
ABERGORLECH

Trawscoed

⑤

N

1 km

1 mile

② Nant Llywelau-bach

③
④
⑥
⑦

Afon Gorlech

①

to
Llansawel

ABERGORLECH

B4310

⑧ START
picnic site

to Carmarthen

help here) and gain perhaps the most charming section of the walk.

The path swings left from the ford and follows the western side of the valley, climbing slightly as it goes. On reaching a blue waymark post after about half a mile, take the narrow grassy path to your left. At the next blue waymark and junction, again bear left and down on a sometimes muddy path which leads you to a third path junction. Here you go straight on along the path signed 'short walk'. This leads you to a track where you bear left by a blue waymark post and a white arrow. The track becomes a surfaced lane as it leads down to the B4310 in Abergorlech.

8. Turn right to visit the bridge, the pub and the best display of 'Gorlech Stones', or left past the village stores to regain the start of the walk at the picnic site.

My profuse thanks to Mike Scott of Forest Enterprise whose knowledgeable and friendly help and advice were invaluable in putting this walk together.

2: Brechfa

Distance: 4½ miles (7.3 km)

Time: 3 hours

Maps: OS Landranger 146 Lampeter and Llandovery and OS Pathfinder 1035 Pencader and 1059 Carmarthen.

Start: Victoria Park picnic site, by the village hall, opposite the church 524 302. Public toilets.

Terrain: Mainly on good paths and lanes. Steep at start. Muddy in places.

Nearest Towns: Carmarthen and Llandeilo.

Parking: See Start

Refreshments: The Forest Arms Hotel (an excellent pub), Ty Mawr Country House Hotel and Restaurant, Glasfryn Guest House and Restaurant (cream teas), PO shop.

Stiles: 8

Suitable for: All. Dogs on leads through farmland please.

Along the way

Brechfa is a small village that gives its name to the sprawling, and mostly coniferous p   lantation, Brechfa Forest. In the Middle Ages the forest of oak and ash was an important hunting ground and Brechfa itself provided accommodation for the royal and noble hunters. During the First World War a factory in the village used local wood to produce naphtha for the explosives industry, while wood from the forest provided fuel and materials for the South Wales industrial revolution.

The Church of St Teilo in the centre of the village is fairly modern, having been built in 1893 to replace the small and dilapidated original building that dated back (in part) to the sixth century. Parts of the old building were included in the new and the present church

Afon Cothi, Brechfa

has a very pleasant and welcoming atmosphere. The church in Brechfa has a fascinating history, being founded by St Teilo and, at times, serving as a grange of Talley Abbey and having some very sporting rectors.

One of these, Joshua Davies, was appointed to the living of Brechfa for having agreed to take the place of a missing team member for an important football match. He was fond of both football – played in a field by the church – and the occasional beer, on which subject he is quoted as saying, 'Don't do as I do, do as I say.'

It is reported that another rector, Thomas Jones, often had to be summoned back for Evensong from his salmon fishing by the furious ringing of the church bells. It was not until after the First World War that the triple bell cote was filled, a new bell from the chemical works joining the bell from the old church and a bell specially made for the new church.

Although seemingly a backwater, Brechfa has been involved in great world affairs. In the 1930s a camp was built locally for unemployed workers from the South Wales valleys. Open from March to September each year, the camp provided accommodation for the men sent to build roads for the Forestry Commission. During the Spanish Civil War it was used to house Basque refugee children. A detailed history 'Teulu Teilo', a History of the Church in Brechfa is available in the church and is well-written and amusing, giving an insight into the life of this quiet village.

The walk itself heads to the south of the village, avoiding the coniferous plantations of Brechfa Forest, climbing over Banc y Daren to give superb views, including those over the Cothi and Marlais valleys. Much of the walk is shaded by the oak and ash of the old Brechfa Forest, while naturalists will find the variety of wild life and flowers fascinating. The hedgerows are full of colour with wood anemone, celandine, hart's-tongue fern, wood sage, wild strawberries and other plants to be seen. The trees are covered in lichens and mosses, while an area of wet grassland near the end of the walk has marsh-loving plants including meadowsweet, spotted orchids, bog asphodel, wild angelica and ragged robin growing amid tussock grass.

The bird life to be found along the way can include buzzards, dippers, wagtails, tree creepers, woodpeckers and, if lucky, red kites and kingfishers. Look out for grey squirrels dashing through the trees, and salmon rising in the river, as well as sign of some of our larger wild mammals in the woods.

The route taken follows what were once important tracks serving the local inhabitants, but are now quiet byways past the ruins of a hafod, or 'summer dwelling', high on the hill once used by shepherds when stock could graze higher land, and a deserted farm at Clyn Llydan, where nature is reclaiming a once substantial dwelling.

The Route

From the car park and picnic site in Victoria Park, where the remains of a dried-up holy well can be seen, return to the road and turn right. Opposite the Forest Arms Hotel, turn left between the rectory and the churchyard and follow the lane down to the ford across the Afon Marlais. There is no footbridge or stepping stones here, but the ford is often shallow enough to splash across dry-footed. If you do not fancy trying this, return to the road, turn left across the bridge and turn left again on a track below the chapel to gain the southern side of the ford.

1. From the ford, the lane known as the Old Road climbs steeply as it

winds southwards up the side of Banc y Daren. Follow it for approximately three-quarters of a mile, ignoring waymarked side turnings, and going sharp left after each of the gates on the road. Although seemingly unending, this climb has compensations in the form of ever-expanding views and, if you do this walk in the summer, wild strawberry picking as you go.

In some places the lane is sunken into the hill, in others it has high hedges, and in yet others open views, but it eventually gets you up to a saddle or pass between Banc y Daren and its neighbouring hill, where the lane turns sharp right and the walk abandons it.

2. At the bend go straight on through a gateway waymarked with the 'Dyfed County Walks' disc, then bear right down the fence line, following a sunken and rather boggy track.

3. This track is followed as it swings left, passes the ruins of Hafod and descends towards the Afon Cothi down a steep-sided stream valley, cloaked in majestic trees. The track is well-graded and a pleasure to walk. Ignore side turns and follow the stream on your right, which is heard more often than seen, until the track brings you down through the farmyard of Ty Llwyd.

4. Just below the farm turn left at a track junction and head northwards to the buildings at Daren Fawr.

5. By Daren Fawr turn left up a waymarked track that leads up alongside the rushing Afon Cothi, and through oak and ash woodland of great beauty. After approximately three-quarters of a mile, the path abandons the river and leads up with a wooded bank on your left and a fence on your right, to a gate.

6. Go through the gate, then left up the waymarked track that swings around the north-west side of the ruins of Clyn Llydan and between fields, down to cross the Afon Marlais on a rather elderly and decrepit gated footbridge by an ancient ford that has lasted better.

Safely across the footbridge, turn left across the track cut into the rock leading to the ford, and up to a stile. Cross this into a field

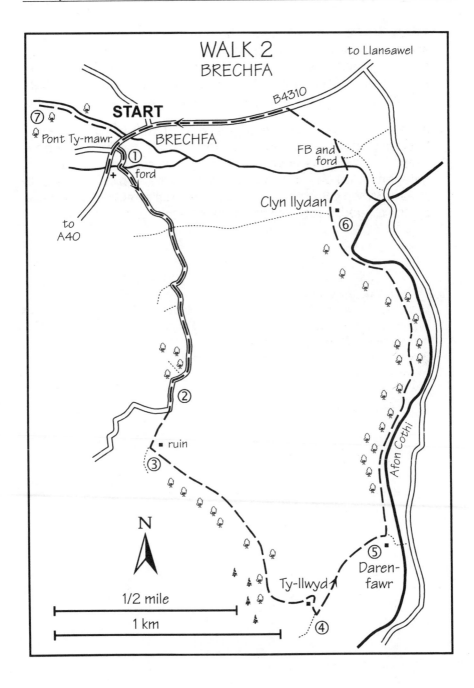

WALK 2
BRECHFA

to Llansawel

START

Pont Ty-mawr

BRECHFA

B4310

FB and ford

ford

to A40

Clyn llydan

⑥

①

⑦

Afon Cothi

②

ruin

③

N

⑤ Daren-fawr

Ty-llwyd

④

1/2 mile

1 km

where a faint path leads you through the scrubby margins and across the flower-rich wet grassland to a gap near the middle of the top northern hedge. Cross the next field diagonally left to a stile and gate on to the B4310. Turn left and walk back down through Brechfa to the start of the walk at Victoria Gardens.

7. A pleasant riverside walk of slightly more than half a mile in total, through oak woods bordering the Afon Marlais, can be enjoyed by simply following the river side of the picnic site up to a hunter's gate, and then on a narrow path alongside the highly attractive stream. When you come to a fence with no stile, retrace your steps by this rugged, deep-cut stream back to the start of the walk.

3: Caio

Distance: 8½ miles (13.8 km)

Time: 4 to 5 hours

Maps: OS Landranger 146 Lampeter, Llandovery and Surrounding Area, Pathfinder 1013 Cilycwm and Pumsaint.

Start: Caio 675 398

Terrain: Mainly good tracks – one stretch of about 1½ miles of almost trackless, rough hillwalking – one tough uphill climb – some road walking. Muddy/boggy in places.

Nearest Town: Llandovery

Parking: Roadside parking opposite school in Caio

Public Transport: None

Refreshments: Brunant Arms, Caio

Stiles: 3

Suitable for: Those prepared for rough walking. The hilltop section is hard going and in bad weather should not be undertaken by those who cannot be sure of accurate use of a map and compass. The Pathfinder map is almost essential for accurate navigation here. Dogs on leads through farmland, please.

Along the way

This walk takes in some wild terrain, with superb views over the Co-thi Valley, forestry and farmland. Man's current usage of these hills is plain to see, while evidence of man's more ancient presence is also to be found.

As you reach the road just below Glan-Meddyg, you cross the line of a Roman aqueduct (although little sign of it can actually be seen on the ground), and most of the paths used on this walk date back to the dim and distant past and may even pre-date the Roman occupation of the region. Certainly the track up on to the hills from Cwrt y Cadno was once an important route over the hills to Cilycwm and the Tywi Valley, and the summits around have a good sprinkling of ancient cairns and standing stones.

The modern Caio forest is an extensive conifer plantation, and while the forestry tracks followed on this walk mainly follow the line of ancient paths, in places forestry needs and historical rights of way diverge. Unfortunately one stretch of footpath is now overgrown, but easily bypassed on a good forestry track. In many places the conifers are young enough (at the time of writing) to allow good views over their tops, while in others the uninspiring monoculture is fringed with oaks, ash and other broadleaved trees, making a more pleasant environment for wildlife and walkers alike.

Beneath its modern surface appearance, this is an ancient and beautiful landscape and it is not hard to imagine how wild it was in Twm Shon Catti's day (the local, Welsh Robin Hood who roamed these hills), or even during the tribal Celtic and Roman eras.

The Dolaucothi Roman Gold Mines at nearby Pumsaint have an excellent exhibition on the history of the mines and local area and are well worth a visit after your walk. Organised tours are available for visits to both the ancient and more modern workings. For more information on the National Trust-owned Dolaucothi Mines, telephone 01558 650359.

The Route

From the car parking area opposite the school in Caio, head up northward past the church with its elaborate lych-gate. At the junction by the Brunant Arms where the road turns sharp right, go straight on up the lane signposted 'Picnic Site'. This takes you up past attractive cottages to a junction of unsurfaced tracks by some corrugated metal sheds. Go left here, again following the sign 'Picnic Site', and follow the track down towards the Afon Annell. Nearing the river, the track again divides and our route goes left and left again down to a footbridge (built on the site of an older vehicular bridge) and ford, across the river to the picnic site.

On the other side of the picnic site you come to a major junction of tracks. Take the one straight on and uphill. This well-graded right of

The Upper Cothi Valley above Cwrt y Cadno

way now climbs for approximately three-quarters of a mile in an almost straight line and at an almost constant gradient (ignore any side turnings), to reach the crest of a ridge and the end of the forestry at the same time. Although the climb can prove tiring, the view you meet by the gate and stile out of the forestry makes it all worthwhile, as you look out over the Cothi Valley to the hills beyond.

1. Cross into the field and, on almost the same heading as before, cross the top corner of the field to an obvious gate. Go through this and follow the left-hand fence of the field you have now entered. As you approach the gate in the far corner, you find you are in a slightly sunken trackway and the nearer you get to the farm below, passing through several gateways as you go, the more obvious and well-used the ancient, but still used track becomes.

Entering this well-kept and neat farm, you cross a small stream where it can prove muddy underfoot, but below the farm there is an excellent unsurfaced track which zigzags down to the road. In the trees on your right as you reach the road are the remains of a Ro-

man aqueduct. Unfortunately, these are not readily visible, although the aqueduct has been traced for some distance along the
south-east side of the valley.

2. Turn right along the road, drop down to and cross the Afon Cothi
   and follow this quiet country lane along the valley for about one
   and a quarter miles, until, just past the impressive chapel at Cwrt-
   y-Cadno, you take a right turn down a lane signed as a 'No
   Through Road'.

3. This takes you down to, and back across, the Afon Cothi, then up
   sharply to a junction with an unsurfaced track. Turn right along the
   track, then almost immediately left. This has the appearance of a
   private drive and takes you up to a charming cottage. The right of
   way goes straight on between the cottage and the old stable block,
   up across a steep lawn to a gate on the other side of the garden.
   Please respect the privacy of the cottage residents and cross their
   garden as unobtrusively and as quietly as you can to minimise any
   disturbance to them.

4. Once through the gate out of the garden, the route zigzags steeply
   up a rough grassy track over a knoll, then follows the right-hand
   fence up to a gate in the top right-hand corner of a field. Through
   the gate, a short section of old green lane leads you onto a good
   track that takes you up a spur, through several gateways, past a
   sheepfold and eventually to a gateway on to the open hill.

5. The actual right of way diverges from the track a little before this
   gateway and drops down to the east corner of the fences to cross,
   then follow the fence for some 200 metres before dropping down
   to the Rhyd Ddu Ford. This route, however, is difficult to find and
   there is no stile in the fence, so it may be more acceptable to follow
   the track to the gateway, go through and turn right following a faint
   and often boggy track south-south-east to the ford.

   Near the gate are some large rocks, held by some to be fallen
   'standing stones' or route markers. The ford can prove very awkward for walkers as it is fairly deep, wide and boggy, and is in my
   experience best crossed upstream, using tussocks of reed grass

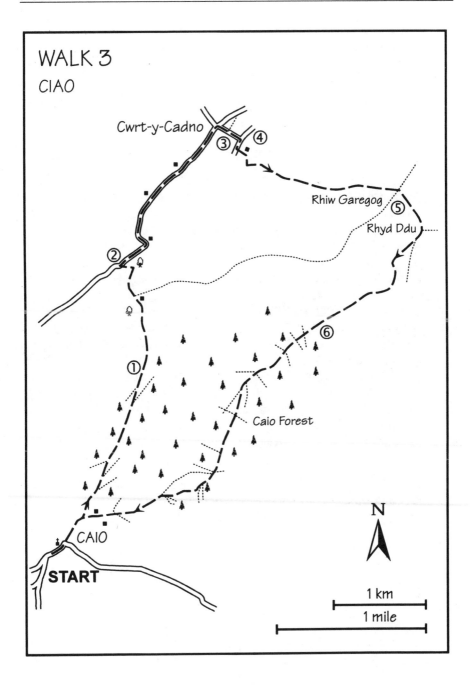

WALK 3
CIAO

Cwrt-y-Cadno

Rhiw Garegog

Rhyd Ddu

Caio Forest

CAIO

START

N

1 km

1 mile

as stepping stones, or by hurrying across where previous crossings have made a mat of grass. Gaiters will help keep feet dry!

Once across the ford, head in a generally south-westerly direction
on a faint trackway skirting the bog. It is easy here to miss or wander off the right of way, but if you do lose the path you want to head
roughly south-west from the ford, skirting the bog that feeds the
Afon Annell, heading for the forestry some 300 metres south of the
small gorge that empties the bog.

All being well, you will find the first ancient and faint trackway
which will lead you up to a more obvious one. This is mainly notice-
able as a half-filled-in ditch with clumps of reed grass and pools of
bog, that lies parallel to the stream emptying the main bog and
some 200 to 250 metres uphill south-east of it. This leads you directly to a gate into the forestry of the Caio Forest and onto an excellent track. This can be rather muddy at the gateway.

6. Follow this forestry track roughly south-west for approximately
    two-thirds of a mile, down to a fork in the track, ignoring any side
    turnings. Take the left fork, which leads more southerly, and follow
    this for about another two-thirds of a mile to another fork, where
    the route goes right. The track heads first south-west and then
    more west and you follow it for approximately 600 metres, ignoring
    any side turns, down to a staggered crossroads. Here you go
    straight over (or as it may also be described 'second left') into a
    track that leaves the forest and drops down between thickly
    hedged fields.

    Follow this track down for some 900 metres, ignoring side turns,
    past a couple of farms to the T-junction with the corrugated metal
    sheds you passed near the start of the walk. Turn left and descend
    into Caio, the pub and your car.

4: Cenarth and Newcastle Emlyn

Distance: 4 miles (6.5km)

Time: 2 hours

Maps: OS Landranger 145 Cardigan and Surrounding Area, OS Pathfinder 1011 Newcastle Emlyn

Start: Cenarth Bridge 269 415

Terrain: Mainly green lanes, lanes and good paths. Can be rather overgrown and/or muddy in places. I recommend carrying a stick to beat down brambles.

Nearest Town: Newcastle Emlyn

Parking: Cenarth: Small free car park on Carmarthen side of the river, 50 metres along the Boncath road, or large car park (not free) on the Ceredigion side of the river at the end of the bridge. Newcastle Emlyn: Large mart car park or smaller car park by castle. Both get very full on Fridays (Mart Day), when the third car park, off the Carmarthen Road, may prove emptier.

Refreshments: Pubs, cafés and shops at both Cenarth and Newcastle Emlyn.

Stiles: Two – both currently in poor condition

Suitable for: All. Dogs on leads across farmland, please, and no dogs in the castle grounds.

Along the way

This walk follows a linear route joining two fascinating 'border outposts', both of which have great atmosphere and show remains of their historical importance. The walk starts at Cenarth, famous for its waterfall, bridge and the National Coracle Centre, then follows the 'old road', now downgraded to bridleway and footpath status, to

Newcastle Emlyn, a quiet market town with a wonderfully-sited castle.

The bridge at Cenarth is first recorded by Gerald of Wales in 1188, though the present bridge is a later construction built some time around the middle of the 18th century, but Cenarth has been of importance since well before this.

St Llawddog's Church, a very pleasant 19th-century building with a bell turret over a superb rose window, stands on the slope above the bridge and occupies the site of the original church, which was a sixth-century monastic settlement founded by St Llawddog himself. Inside the church is found the unusually decorated bowl of the font which dates no later than the 12th century and has a design of a serpentine ribbon and human faces. Rescued from a Cardiganshire farm where it was being used as a pig trough (!), the bowl was returned to the church in the 19th century.

In the churchyard is found an ancient three-faced, almost conical, millstone grit stone. Known locally as the Gelli Dywyll stone, it was brought to the churchyard for safe keeping in 1896. Before this, the stone's history is confused, some believing it to have come from Parc y Maen Llwyd (Field of the Grey Stone) near the church and taken to Gellidywyll to stand on the mansion's lawn as a headstone or monument to a favourite dead horse, while others will have it that it came from Maenclochog, 10 miles away on the far side of the Preseli Hills. The inscription, which translates to read 'Curcagnus, son of Andagellus' ties it to another stone near Maenclochog which commemorates Andagellus, son of Caveti.

The Three Horseshoes, just below the church, is a 19th-century pub on the site of the old coaching inn, while the original public house, the Old Brewhouse by the present pub, is the oldest building in the village and has been renovated from a sadly dilapidated state. Dating back to mediaeval times, this unpretentious building was probably within the original Christian settlement on this spot. Gerald of Wales could well have supped here!

The 17th-century flour mill, nestling on the river bank below the church, is well worth a visit, as is the National Coracle Centre with its unique collection of coracles not only from Wales, but from around the world. One ticket luckily gives admission to both. Open Easter to the end of October, Sunday to Friday, 10.30 – 5.30, these attractions give an insight into the local historical and worldwide im-

The castle, Newcastle Emlyn

portance of the coracle and a taste of historical flour production. For more information call 01239 710980.

The mill overlooks the famous waterfall and salmon leap where traces of the mediaeval fish traps can still be found, and on certain dates, daredevil canoeists brave the pounding waters of the falls.

A much fuller history of Cenarth is to be found in the booklet *Cenarth Falls* by C Mervyn Thomas. This is highly recommended and available from the Old Smithy Craftshop and Heritage Centre opposite the Three Horseshoes Inn. The Old Smithy has a restored 18th-century blacksmith's forge and other historical displays which are well worth viewing. Also worth seeing are the Norman motte, the sweet water spring, the site of the 'other mill' and the salmon museum. In all, Cenarth is a small, but fascinating place to visit.

Newcastle Emlyn is a market town with an interesting history. Growing up around the river crossing, the town gets its name from the castle that was founded around 1240 by Maredudd ap Rhys, son of Rhys ap Gruffyd, who was responsible for stemming the Norman conquest of Wales for half a century. The castle saw little action, though it was captured in 1403 by Owain Glyndwr, and was a royalist stronghold in the Civil War, eventually being blown up on orders from Cromwell. Nowadays, the ruins are 'consolidated' and are an attractive, and at night spotlit, adjunct to a quiet town. On the north side of the castle, you can see the weir and mill-race used at one time to power a mill and later to provide electricity for the town cinema!

The imposing bulk of the Cawdor Hall at the head of Castle Street houses the library, covered market and Tourist Information Centre, as well as having the town's Council Chamber and the Attic Theatre on the first floor. The Attic Players is one of the area's amateur dramatic societies, putting on several plays and shows each year, including their annual panto which is always popular with audiences young and old. Oh no it isn't. **Oh yes it is!**

An attractive bridge crosses the Teifi to Adpar, where the first printing press in Wales was set up just opposite the end of the bridge, while the river itself saw the demise of the last dragon in Wales – supposedly in 1814! It seems that the said dragon was terrorising the town until one Rhys of Hendre, a veteran just returned from the Peninsular campaigns against Napoleon, saved the town by shooting it. Using a red shawl as cover, Rhys waded into the river and shot the dragon as it rested on the castle walls. Dreadfully wounded, the dragon fell on the shawl and ripped it in its death throes, while Rhys swam to shore safe and well. It is said the dragon's blood and venom stained the river red and green, poisoning the water for a full year. However, this story could have an earlier basis in the fall of the castle in 1403, when Sir Thomas Carew threw Owain Glyndwr's red and green banner into the river.

1814 did, however, see one historic death, that of Thomas Heslop at the hands of 'gentle' John Beynon in what is regarded as 'the last duel in Wales'. The tombstone of the loser has an inscription 'Alas Poor Heslop'.

Once an important centre for the droving of pigs and cattle, Newcastle Emlyn boasted over 30 pubs along the three-quarter mile of the town's streets. A good number remain and offer even the thirstiest walker the chance to quench his thirst.

Although the walk described is linear, you have a choice of return journey: by the regular bus services, by walking back the way you came, or by walking back along quiet lanes south of the main road.

Clever walkers with cars to spare will leave a car at each end to facilitate the return trip.

The Route

From Cenarth Bridge, follow the main road towards Newcastle Emlyn for approximately 100 metres until you come to the Three Horseshoes Inn. Turn left and pass between the main building and The Old Brewhouse to reach the inn's car park.

1. From the car park follow the narrow path alongside the church wall and past the old school (now flats) to meet the end of a tarmac lane. Bear left, then turn right just before the gates to a house with wooden shingles, down a rather neglected green lane. The short section of green lane leads you into a field where you follow the right-hand hedge up to a gate in the corner. The motte above Cenarth is clearly visible from this field.

   The gate opens into a section of farm track which takes you past Old Vicarage Farm, but where the track turns sharp right 100 metres beyond the farm, go straight ahead through gated pens into a green lane. This section of the green lane, the old Newcastle Emlyn to Cenarth Road, can prove rather overgrown for the next 500 metres, but eventually meets the lane to Gillo Fach.

2. Turn right and follow the lane to the main road which, by a trick of perspective, is almost invisible until you reach it. Cross the road with care and go up the drive to Gillo Farm opposite. Just before entering the farmyard, bear left and go through the gate by the 'farm shop' sign into a very attractive section of green lane.

3. At the widening of the lane by an old quarry, follow the left-hand fence to the corner, where you cross by the most rudimentary of stiles to follow the obvious and slightly sunken green lane ahead. Passing some magnificent old and storm-wracked beech trees (where the path can again prove rather overgrown for a short distance), you come to a fence. This can be by-passed by going left to a gate back on to the green lane. The views back towards Cenarth are superb from this spot.

The green lane leads down past the magnificent, though neglected farm buildings of Gelligatti and the very attractive house,
and becomes a surfaced lane.

4. Follow the lane for just over half a mile, down to a T-junction of
   quiet lanes where you turn right. After about 350 metres, turn left
   down a rough track, the bedrock surface of which can be very slippery when wet, to Cwm Sarah. The track zigzags steeply down to
   a ford and footbridge in the bottom of the cwm, where the number
   of hippies living here once earned this charming spot the name
   'Hippy Valley'. Go up the other side and on to meet the road just
   below Newcastle Emlyn School.

5. Turn left down to the A484 where you turn right. After 50 metres
   turn left down Porth Street to Fountain Square. Here the Town
   Council have erected a reconstructed horse trough. Turn left and
   follow the initially wide main street for about 300 metres, past
   shops and banks down to Cawdor Hall with its attractive clock
   tower. Turn right up the 'no entry' street following signs 'to the Castle'.

   Rather than go straight up Castle Street to the ruins, turn right opposite the Neuadd Emlyn Hall and drop down by the steps next to
   the flag poles to gain the riverside walk. This follows the riverside
   in a loop around and beyond the castle, eventually leading back
   alongside the mill-race and up to the castle entrance.

6. It is worth turning left here to explore the ruins before passing
   through the gates into Castle Street. Just by the gates are the site
   of an ancient chapel and an interesting interpretation board giving
   the castle's history.

   Follow the attractively flagged and cobbled Castle Street past the
   Catholic church and back to the Cawdor Hall, taking the right hand
   fork to pass the Tourist Information Office and rejoin the main
   street. Turn left, then immediately right down the road opposite the
   Cawdor Hall and follow this past Bethel Chapel and the Old Court
   House to the attractive Holy Trinity Church. Unfortunately, the
   church is normally kept locked, but the south wall has an interest-

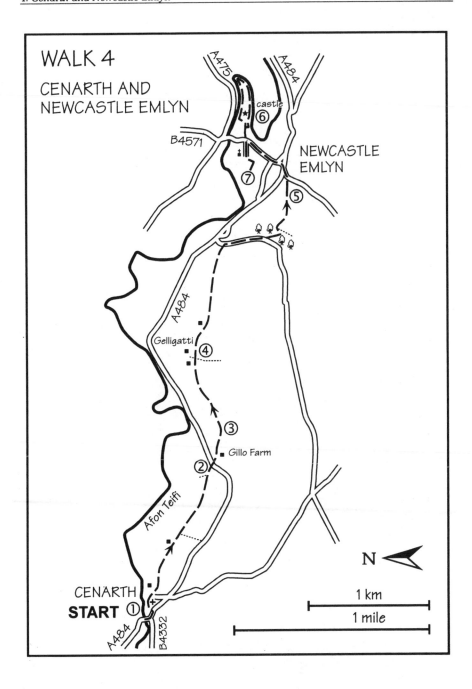

WALK 4

CENARTH AND
NEWCASTLE EMLYN

ing memorial sundial and the churchyard is well-kept and peaceful.

Just beyond the church the road turns sharp left and runs along the side of the playing fields, rapidly narrowing to a footpath which takes you up to the Mart.

7. On reaching the Mart, turn right and you soon find yourself in the Mart Car Park, the end of the walk.

5: Drefach Felindre

Distance: 4½ miles (7.25 km)

Time: 2 to 3 hours

Maps: OS Landranger 145 Cardigan and Surrounding Area, OS Pathfinder 1034 Boncath, Capel Iwan and Rhos.

Start: Museum of the Welsh Woollen Industry, Drefach Felindre 355 390

Terrain: Good paths, tracks and quiet roads – muddy in places.

Nearest Town: Newcastle Emlyn

Parking: Roadside in Drefach Felindre

Refreshments: Shop and café at the museum, New Shop Inn and shop in the village.

Public Transport: Scant service from Newcastle Emlyn

Stiles: 2

Suitable for: All. Dogs on leads through farmland.

Along the way

Drefach Felindre was, until recent times, an important producer of Welsh flannel, boasting in 1900 that no parish in Wales produced more flannel. Now the industry has all but vanished, leaving only traces, with the stream sides still bearing witness to the passing of the once all-powerful woollen mills, with leats and dams, as well as ex-mills, converted and derelict.

1994 saw the start of an interesting project to identify from census documents all the buildings of the area used in the woollen industry. The footpaths around the area were then cleared to form a network of walking trails that link the various sites and pass through some beautiful scenery. Over 130 buildings were identified and 57 rights of way cleared, totalling over 24 miles of paths.

The workforce used in the project included members of the Brit-

Museum of the Welsh Woollen Industry, Drefach Felindre

ish Trust for Conservation Volunteers and the United National Association – International Youth Service, with workers in the teams coming from Holland, Germany, France, Denmark, Italy, Canada, Slovakia and Japan, as well as Britain. This has made it possible to enjoy informative and attractive walks in what was once a heavily industrialised area and which is now a quiet, rural backwater.

Map leaflets, available in Tourist Information offices, entitled Llwybrau'r Gwlan Woollen Trails, give much more detail of the project, identifying all the buildings involved in the woollen industry, showing the cleared paths and giving historical notes. Information panels in each village provide more local detail. It should be noted that, at the time of writing, not all the marked paths are totally clear and waymarking is not completely finished, while the cleared paths do not always follow the rights of way as shown on the OS maps.

There is extensive evidence of a diverse wildlife in the area, from grey squirrels in the trees and other large wild mammals to buzzards soaring on thermals above. Wild flowers abound, bluebells being found in profusion in the woods.

The village was the scene of violence during the famous 'Rebecca

Riots' when toll gates and other unpopular symbols of 'unfair exploi-
tation' of the working classes were destroyed, in various parts of
West Wales, by men disguised as women – 'Rebecca and her Daugh-
ters'! The toll gate in Drefach Felindre took a mere fifteen minutes to
destroy and the gatekeeper was run off. No rioters seem to have been
identified or apprehended for this action.

The walk starts and finishes at the Museum of the Welsh Woollen
Industry, which is well worth a visit. Housed in the Cambrian Mill,
this fascinating working museum has a full working mill on site, Me-
lin Teifi, working entirely towards modern production, and showing the history of the local woollen industry in an easily understood
and interesting way. The Museum's visitor guide points out various
mills in the area – naming and giving the history of many sites
passed on the walk, as well as having three interesting self-guided
trails of its own. The guide is well worth carrying on the walk, giving
more details than I can fit in here.

The Route

1. The walk starts by leaving the road down a track beside and paral-
    lel to the entrance to the museum (which you should make a point
    of visiting), and follows a clear route through a wooden gate. When
    the track swings sharply to the right, go straight on through a metal
    gate and down a grass track to a quiet road.

2. Turn right past the site of a former mill, now a leisure centre (note
    the murals on the walls), and up a steep road for approximately
    100 metres to a track on the left. Take this track, which climbs then
    dips down to some houses where you turn left along the drive to
    the road. Cross and take the track almost directly opposite, bear-
    ing right at a track junction through Dandinas farmyard and into the
    woods above the stream that once powered five mills.

    Continue along the track past the almost invisible remains of Pant
    y Barcud Mill and on coming to a small white cottage, take the now
    narrow footpath along the right-hand side of the building.

3. Follow the side of the stream over a muddy tributary spring by a
    footbridge, then cross the stream by a footbridge over a rocky wa-

terfall to the side of a now silted-up and overgrown pond. This pond was once a header reservoir for the mills. The path crosses by way of the old dam wall, crossing the overflow cut into the rock by a third footbridge, before swinging right and climbing up past a cottage to a wide track. Turn left, away from an attractive ford, to gain the road. Turn right along this quiet lane to Cwmhiraeth.

4. At the road junction turn right and follow the road into the hamlet, once home to more mills. A leat once ran through what are now the front gardens of cottages on the right-hand side of the road. Just before reaching the bridge, take the track up to the left, signed Troed-y-Rhiw. Follow this, skirting left above the houses 600 metres up the track, to a track crossroads. Go straight on roughly south-east to reach the road.

Follow the road straight on and left at a sharp bend, then leave it 100 metres past the bend for a track running down to the right. This takes you down past Mynwent Soar Cemetery to Penlangribin.

5. Just before you reach the farm, the track swings sharp left and the walk leaves it over a waymarked stile to the right, next to a gate, right on the corner. Having crossed into the field, turn left and follow the boundary down to a stile in the corner.

From here the path zigzags down, through a kissing gate and down some steps to meet a broad path. Turn left and follow this path below the farm and through woodland, across a broad track down to a small stream. Cross the stream and climb up to a path junction, where you turn right and follow the often muddy path to a gate and stile into a rather marshy field. Go straight across the field to gain the road by way of a footbridge over a stream and a good stile.

Once on this quiet road, turn left and follow it down past five more old mill buildings into Drefach Felindre. Follow the road over the bridge into the centre of the village, then turn right opposite St Barnabas Church. Go along the road past many old buildings once associated with the woollen trade, back to the start of the walk at the museum.

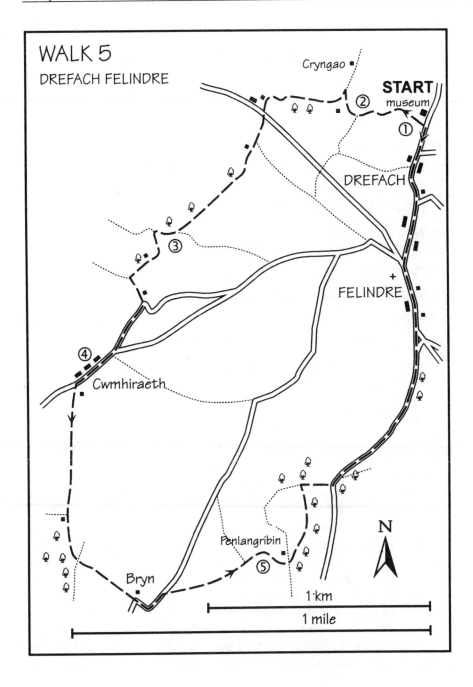

WALK 5
DREFACH FELINDRE

Cryngao

START
museum

② ①

DREFACH

DREFACH

③

+
FELINDRE

④
Cwmhiraeth

Penlangribin

⑤

Bryn

N

1·km
1 mile

6: Drefelin and Cwmpengraig

Distance: 4 miles (6.5 km)

Time: 2 to 3 hours

Maps: OS Landranger 145 Cardigan, OS Pathfinder 1034 Boncath, Capel Iwan and Rhos.

Start: Information panel in Drefelin, 361 380

Terrain: Mainly well-maintained woodland footpaths and field paths, several steep climbs. Good waymarking.

Nearest Town: Newcastle Emlyn

Parking: Limited roadside parking in Drefelin

Refreshments: None

Stiles: 13 – many built with only the long-legged in mind!

Suitable for: All. Dogs on leads through farmland.

Along the way

This area of Carmarthenshire was, until recent times, an important producer of Welsh flannel. See the introduction to Walk 5 for details of an interesting project to identify and record the buildings which were used in the industry, and to construct trails which link the sites.

The walk described starts in Drefelin where, at one time or another, 11 buildings were used in the woollen industry, ranging from small rural mills to specialist weavers, from yarn spinners to hand-loom workshops; and takes in Cwmpengraig where 14 buildings were once involved in the industry, every facet from stocking knit-ting to specialist weaving being represented.

Penboyr Church, visited on the route, is an unassuming building on a historical site, perhaps dating back to Roman times, and is next to the hump of Tomenlawddog, an ancient, though small, motte and

Old mill, Drefelin

bailey castle. The views from this and many other spots on the route are extensive, while a large part of the walk is through mainly oak woods that cling to the steep sides of the valleys above the rushing streams that once powered the woollen mills.

There is an enormous variety of wildlife in the area, from grey squirrels in the trees and other large wild mammals to buzzards soaring on thermals above. Bluebells, particularly, can be found in profusion in the woods, but there are many other wild flowers to enjoy on this walk.

A visit to the Museum of the Welsh Woollen Industry in nearby Drefach is recommended for all who find the history of the area and its industry of interest.

The Route

From the information panel in Drefelin, head east up the road follow-ing the valley of the Nant Bargod for some 400 metres until, just past the imposing chapel, you come to a telephone kiosk.

1. Almost directly opposite is a footbridge over the Nant Wthan. Cross this and follow the left-hand hedge around farm buildings down to a kissing gate, which leads to a second footbridge. After crossing, bear left to yet another footbridge which leads you across the Nant Bargod and up a path over a small crag. Note how the steps, cut into the living rock, are still in good condition, but the iron handrail is rusted to a dangerous state of disrepair. The path then bears left up the craggy spur to a T-junction of paths with a waymark post. Go straight on, enjoying impressive views as the path hugs the top of the Bargod Valley.

2. Coming to a fork in the wide path just beyond a gate and stile some 300 metres further on, take the left, downhill option. Ignore any paths coming in from the left and after approximately 600 metres you come to a small stream. Splash across this, then on entering a field bear hard right, crossing the field up to a stile almost hidden in the trees opposite. A stiff climb, straight ahead, along the fence on your left, takes you to the valley rim again and a stile into the woods.

3. Follow the track through the top of the woods for about 250 metres to where you cross a stile. Here, by a spring, you turn right into a green lane which is followed for some 600 metres. Just before the lane reaches a farm, take the stile on your right, which is clearly waymarked, and drop down to a waymark post on a track in the field. Turn left and follow the track to a gate and stile on to the quiet lane. Turn left and follow the lane up to Tomenlawddog motte and bailey castle and Penboyr church to enjoy superb views.

4. From the church, retrace your steps past the farm and along the lane to a T-junction.

Turn left here, then after 50 metres abandon the surfaced lane for a waymarked track down to your right. Follow this track, which be-

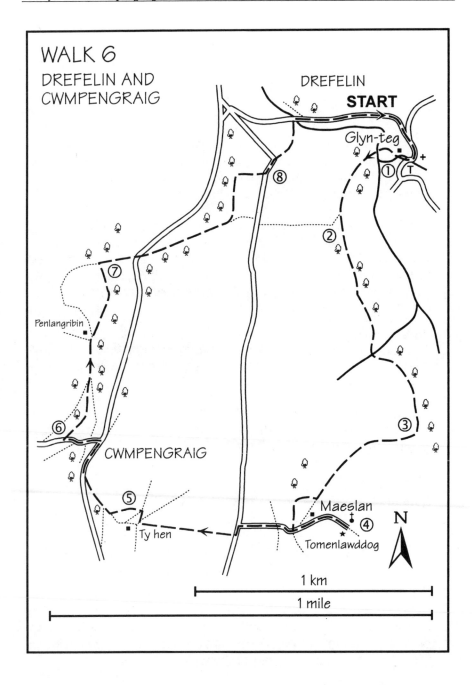

comes a green lane after passing some sheep pens, to just above the buildings of Ty Hen, where you turn right over a waymarked stile to follow a waymarked path that circles around the house and garden through newly planted hardwood saplings.

5. Crossing a stile below the house you come to a rough track, but this is abandoned almost immediately as you cross a stile on your right which puts you on a path that zigzags down through the trees to the road just above Cwmpengraig. Turn right and follow the road into the village and down to a crossroads. Turn left, cross the stream and follow the lane uphill back into woodland.

6. A flight of concrete steps on your right leads you up to a kissing gate and to a path through the woods that gives excellent views of the village below. Follow this for some 300 metres as it zigzags through the trees then, meeting another path just after a kissing gate, turn right (downhill), and almost immediately left through another kissing gate.

    Stay on this path as it climbs to just below Penlangribin. Ignore the steps to your left and go on through yet another kissing gate ahead. This leads down through another kissing gate, across a stream and to a T-junction of paths.

7. Go right here and follow the path over a stile, out of the woods and into a field. Drop down across the field, over a bridge over the stream and up to the lane. Turn left, then almost immediately take the waymarked path right which you follow as it zigzags up through the woods.

    Eventually you reach a stile into a field. Cross this field, following the right-hand boundary, to a stile on to a lane.

8. Turn left and follow the lane to just below a bend, where the way-marked path leaves the tarmac surface to zigzag steeply down towards Drefelin.

    At the bottom of the bank, turn left and cross a stile into a field. This is crossed to an obvious stone stile by the bridge ahead and then on to the road in Drefelin. Turn right and follow the road through the village to regain the start of the walk.

7: Eastern Talley

Distance: 8 miles (13 km)

Time: 5 hours

Maps: OS Landranger 146 Lampeter Llandovery and Surrounding Area, OS Pathfinder 1036 Llandovery.

Start: Talley Abbey 632 327

Terrain: Mainly good field paths – can be muddy in places. Old drovers' roads, some road walking, some rather overgrown stretches.

Nearest Town: Llandeilo

Parking: Limited parking at start of walk. Toilets nearby. Alternative lay-by parking at 633 333.

Public Transport: 2 buses per week from Llandeilo!

Refreshments: Pub, tea rooms and post office in Talley.

Stiles: 18 – many poor and awkward.

Suitable for: All. This walk is not very suitable for dogs that are not agile as some stiles would be difficult for them. Dogs on leads, please.

Thanks to: Mr and Mrs Smithers of Aberdauddwr, Llansaron, who have allowed me to include a permissive diversion from the right of way through their property. This diversion not only preserves Mr and Mrs Smithers' privacy, but also gives superior walking. Please do nothing to jeopardise the use of this diversion. Please do not disturb the occupants of the house, and please take care of any stock in the fields. If possible, walking parties should warn Mr and Mrs Smithers of their intention to use this route.

Along the way

This walk, though mainly notable for its stupendous views that

On the Roman Road above Talley

stretch from the Brecon Beacons and Carmarthen Fans to way across Mid Wales, also takes in many points of historical and wildlife interest. As you park by the ruined abbey, it is interesting to note a few facts about these remains.

Founded in the 12th century by Lord Rhys, Talley Abbey was home to monks of the Premonstratensian order (named after the town in France – Premontre – where they originated) for over 400 years. The fate of the abbey was sealed by the Dissolution of the Monasteries ordered by Henry VIII, and in 1537 the abbey closed. The building was used until 1772 as the parish church, when it was found to be unsafe. A new church, St Michael's, a much plainer structure, was built next door and opened in 1773.

Judging from the stone found in many of the old buildings in the quiet and peaceful village, the ruins were used for many years as a ready source of stone for any building works being undertaken, and although there are large quarries further up the B4302, the secluded, wooded hills above Talley are not so scarred.

The Welsh name for Talley is Talyllchau, which means 'head of the lakes' and, indeed, the twin lakes, which lie in glacial hollows, are a major feature of the area. Separated by a narrow, wooded strip of land on which stands Talley Mound, a mediaeval motte, the lakes, designated a Site of Special Scientific Interest, offer a range of aquatic habitats from open water through reed swamp to alder and willow carr. Many types of rare plants, a variety of water fowl, fish, amphibians and invertebrates – including leeches – are to be found here, while the summer flowering of both yellow and white water-lilies form a stunning view. There is no public access to the lakes, but the Dyfed Wildlife Trust, who lease them from the Royal Society for the Protection of Birds, does occasionally give guided walks. For more information telephone 01437 765462.

The rest of the walk passes much of interest to the nature lover, being home to many wild flowers, mammals and birds. Man has, as ever, left his mark. Notable remains passed on the route, apart from the abbey, include an ancient burial mound or cairn near Pigyn Shon Nicolas, by a section of track held locally to be the route of a Roman road.

Part of the route is on old drove-roads, while other parts are on quiet lanes fringed with trees and wild flowers in wonderful sur-roundings. This peaceful corner of Carmarthenshire is so tranquil that you can understand the monks settling here for the quiet con-templation of God's wonders.

The Route

From Talley Abbey head south back towards the main road, but at the junction by Talley House turn right up the lane signed 'unsuitable for heavy goods vehicles'.

1. Follow this quiet lane with its superb views of the valley for some 600 metres until, just before a bungalow called Rhyd Galed, you come to a rather overgrown but waymarked path down to your left. Follow this through a gate and down the left hedge of the field be-yond to a waymarked gate and stile. Cross into the next field and follow the left hedge to a gap in the hedge which leads to a track. Turn right and follow the track down and over the culverted Afon Ddu.

2. Immediately after crossing the culvert, turn right and follow the right-hand hedge to a gate and stile by a footbridge over the Afon Ig. Cross the bridge and turn left, following the hedge up to a gate and stile on to a track. Turn right and follow the track past some houses up to the road.

3. Turn right and follow the road, the B4302, for approximately 300 metres, past the school to a track that joins the road from the left just past a post box. Take this track up to the right-hand end of a house and a wired-up gate. Cross this and follow a rather neglected and overgrown grassy track up to where it would open into a field if it was not blocked by barbed wire and sheep fencing.

    Cross into the field as best you can (there is a gate up to your right) and follow the left boundary up to the far corner. Cross the crude stile here and turn right with the fence on your right side.

4. The route follows this boundary line for some one and a half miles as it climbs and follows the ridge between the Afon Ig and Pyle Bach, crossing many old hedge banks and fences as it goes. The views open up as you climb, giving stunning vistas, firstly over the Brecon Beacons National Park and then over the 'Mid Wales Wilderness'. After approximately three-quarters of a mile, a difficult crossing is made over a totally inadequate stile. You will recognise this point as there is a double fence and a newly planted hedge in front of you, while on the far side of the fence you are following there is a good gate allowing progress along the ridge line.

    Follow this fence, now on your left, for about 300 metres, to where a gate is set in a zigzag in the fence line. Go through this and keep the fence on your right. This eventually leads down to a stile to a short wide track (or deeply inset gateway entrance).

5. Turn left to a surfaced lane, then right along the lane to a junction. Turn left and follow the lane down to Carmel Chapel. At the junction between the Chapel and Blaen y Cwm Farm, turn right and follow the lane for some 800 metres.

6. Just beyond the garage and before the house of Aberdauddwr, follow the permissive diversion around the house by going through

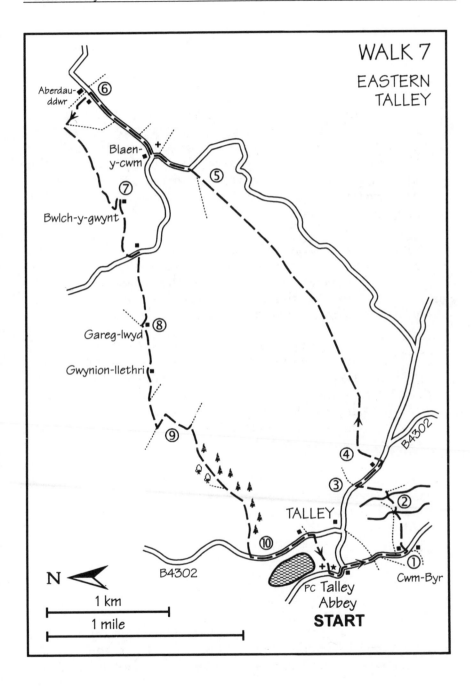

WALK 7
EASTERN
TALLEY

Aberdau-
ddwr

⑥

Blaen-
y-cwm

⑤

⑦

Bwlch-y-gwynt

Gareg-lwyd ⑧

Gwynion-llethri

⑨

B4302

④

③

②

TALLEY

⑩

①

Cwm-Byr

N

1 km

1 mile

B4302

PC Talley
Abbey
START

the gate into a field between house and garage. Cross the length of the field to a gateway in the far end. Cross into the left of the two fields beyond the gate and follow the left boundary up to a gate to a track.

Turn right and follow this track up to the ancient ridge route track some 50 metres on. Here again the views open to wide vistas and the ancient burial mound can be seen to your right. However, the route takes you left, following the boundary along the crest of the ridge. This part of the walk is well waymarked with Dyfed County Walks waymarks and the stiles, although somewhat awkward at times, are in good condition.

7. At first the path follows the fence on the left, then crosses onto the right before zigzagging down through Bwlch y Gwynt farmyard and onto a good farm track to a lane. This is below the hillside known as 'The Pulpit' from where 18th-century Nonconformist ministers preached before the days of chapels.

    Turn left and drop down 50 metres to where, just beyond Pen yr Heol Wen, you leave the lane through a gate and stile on your right, to take a well-defined field path along the right-hand hedge down to a gate and stile in the corner. Cross into a small enclosure and go straight on to another gate ahead. Cross into a field and follow the (muddy) left-hand boundary under mature oak trees down to a stile.

8. Drop down diagonally across the field ahead to reach a stile and footbridge over a small stream. After crossing by the bridge, turn right along a very overgrown path through the trees up to the farmyard of Gareg Lwyd. Beware of geese. Cross under the farmhouse to gain the farm track, which is then followed for 500 metres past Gwynion Llethri.

9. On reaching the second of two cattle grids by a sharp right turn in the track, leave the track and climb up left with the hedge on your right, to a gate and stile. Cross these and turn right, following the right hedge round and up until you come to a gate and stile on a rough track. Go right, through the gate, and follow the track down,

alongside some woods, past Parcydilfa to meet the B4302 by the alternative start of the walk in a lay-by.

Turn left and follow this rather busy stretch of road towards Talley for about 600 metres. Where a waymarked, surfaced path joins from the right, just beyond the first cottage of the village, turn right down to an intriguing turnstile gate. Continue past the end of Upper Talley Lake and into the churchyard. Take the left fork through the churchyard with the abbey ruins on your left, and pass through a rather difficult-to-open gate on to the road by the start of the walk.

8: Ferryside

Distance: 10 miles (16 km), with many opportunities to shorten the distance

Time: 5 hours

Maps: OS Landranger 159 Swansea and The Gower, OS Pathfinders 1105 Pendine and 1081 St Clears and Laugharne.

Start: Car park in centre of Ferryside, opposite railway station, 366 103

Terrain: Mainly good paths and tracks. Some road walking. Muddy in places. Gaiters are essential after rain.

Nearest Town: Carmarthen

Parking: See Start

Public Transport: Rail on Cardiff to Fishguard line, bus from Carmarthen or Llanelli.

Refreshments: Shops, pubs and hotel in Ferryside. Pub in Llansaint, The King's Arms, recommended.

Stiles: 33

Suitable for: All dogs on leads please.

Along the way

Ferryside is little more than a village, but surprisingly enough in Wales, a country with few rail links, it has its own main line station. This reflects its one-time popularity with miners and Swindon's railway workers as a holiday resort. While the village still has golden sands and a slipway, its popularity for traditional holidays has not developed, though the walking is superb in this area.

Llansaint, visited on the walk, is probably built on an Iron Age site and has a fine Norman church, possibly fifth century in origin, with a dominating crenellated tower. Note the tower doorway and the opening with stairs well above head height.

Both villages have a history of 'cockling' – up to 600 tonnes per year of this shellfish being gathered from the estuary sands. At one time the saying went, 'Marry a Llansaint bride and marry a fortune,' reflecting how the cash potential of this 'woman's work' could outstrip the men's farming income.

Lugworm diggers at Ferryside with Llansteffan Castle in the distance

The Route

From the car park, go up the road between the Ship Inn and the White Lion Hotel. Do not go up the hill but follow the road along the wall behind the White Lion, continuing straight on where this becomes pedestrianised. Stay on this level for a little more than half a mile, the route varying from road and hard track to a wooded path, until you come to a T-junction with a through road.

1. Turn right then take the first left signed to Llansaint and Kidwelly. Follow this for about 150 metres to the end of the block wall of a property, where you turn up a narrow and steeply-stepped footpath.

2. Crossing a stile, turn right on a new footpath not yet on OS maps and follow the right-hand hedge. Clear waymarks through dense

bushes lead you on over a stream, then up diagonally across a field and onto a clifftop path with superb views over the Tywi Estuary and up the coast. This section of the walk traverses part of the National Trust's property known as Tregonning Hill. Follow this for some 350 metres to a path junction, where you turn left up a track to fields.

3. Turn right uphill to gain a hedge line which you follow, turning into a green lane to a cottage by the end of a surfaced road.

4. Take the stile opposite the cottage and follow the right-hand hedge round the field to a gate into a small field with a pond. Cross this and take the gate out by the head of the pond. Follow the left-hand hedge to Pengay Farm as views open up in front of you of the Gower Peninsular and Pembrey Forest.

5. Go straight through the farmyard, noting the bell tower that holds a bell taken from a Dutch ship wrecked locally in 1760. About 200 metres past the farm, cross a waymarked stile to your right and follow the hedge down into the woods. The indistinct path now follows waymark posts as it zigzags down past a ruin to the road.

6. Turn left, and after about 40 metres cross a most unstile-like stile and climb the path up to your right to join the hedge line at the top of the field. Follow the path with the hedge on your right up to some buildings, then follow the access drive to the road. Turn left up the road to Llansaint, noting the old 'cockle way' track on your right just before entering the village.

7. On the southern wall of the church, note the two stones (one upside down) bearing sixth-century Irish saints' names, then leave the village by the road alongside the post office. At the T-junction go straight on down the gated lane by the signpost. Cross straight over the first field, then diagonally down the second to the hunters' gate on to the road, to the left of the works.

Cross the road into the woods opposite, bearing left on a faint path, up to a field. Follow the left side of the field up to a step stile on to a farm lane and follow this to the right. After 400 metres the lane goes sharp right, but our route goes left over a stile into the

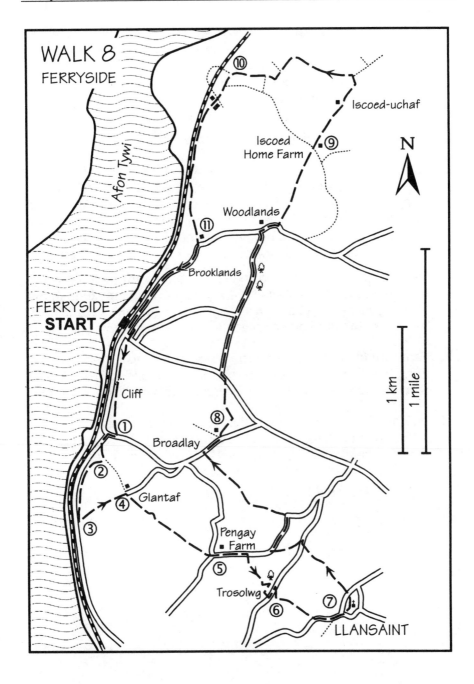

WALK 8
FERRYSIDE

Afon Tywi

⑩

Iscoed-uchaf

Iscoed
Home Farm   ■⑨

N

Woodlands

⑪

Brooklands

FERRYSIDE
START

Cliff

①

⑧

Broadlay

②

④ Glantaf

③

Pengay
■ Farm

⑤

Trosolwg

⑥   ⑦

LLANSAINT

1 km

1 mile

fields – not on the track – and follows first the right hedge for 300 metres to a stile, then the left 250 metres to some trees. Follow the waymarks in a zigzag to a green lane then follow this towards Broadlay. Where the lane veers left to a house, go straight on by stile and hunters' gate to the road.

Turn right and walk on to some attractive houses, turning left by the sign 'Ty Mawr' and following a green lane past more homes.

8. At the end of the green lane, turn left and follow the hedge to a gate, then go diagonally across the next field to the road. Turn left, then first right down a narrow lane and follow this for a little more than three-quarters of a mile to the main road into Ferryside at a T-junction just beyond a bridge. Turn right, then cross and enter fields at a gateway 150 metres on.

As you cross the first field, heading north-north-east, note the partly derelict Iscoed Mansion and ancient standing stone in the field on your right. Follow the right-hand hedge of the second field, then cross the third diagonally to Iscoed Home Farm.

9. Here turn left and follow a green lane to Iscoed Uchaf, then go along this farm lane to a quiet road. Turn left and follow this as it descends towards the estuary, eventually deteriorating to a track.

10. One hundred metres before the rail crossing, go left up a farm track and through the opulent Bronyn, bearing left through the 'farmyard' to gain a metalled track that takes you back towards Ferryside. A modern house is passed with a most unusual miniature village and sculpture garden.

11. On reaching the road, turn right and go over the bridge to regain the start of the walk.

9: Laugharne

Distance: 5 miles (8 km)

Time: 3 hours

Maps: OS Landranger 159 Swansea and the Gower, OS Pathfinders 1105 Pendine and 1081 St Clears and Laugharne.

Start: Foreshore car park 301 106

Terrain: Mainly good paths, tracks and lanes. Steep in places, muddy in others. Foreshore can flood with very high tides.

Nearest Town: Carmarthen

Parking: At start

Refreshments: Cafés, restaurants and pubs (Browns Hotel recommended)

Stiles: 6

Suitable for: All, especially Dylan Thomas fans.

Along the way

It is surprising that Laugharne has no tourist information centre, as coachloads of tourists flock to see the town even out of season due to its international fame as home and burial place of the poet, Dylan Thomas. This walk passes not only the Boat House where Dylan Thomas lived (open to the public during the summer season), his writing shed and his grave, but also gives superb views of the Taf estuary that inspired his writing.

Other points of note on this walk are Laugharne Church, built most probably on an ancient church site, and containing a 10th-century stone cross among many interesting items. The church building, set in an attractive, yew-shaded churchyard, is very handsome and worth a visit.

The castle, which dominates the town, was first built in the 12th

Laugharne Castle

century, though evidence of occupation in the area goes back to the Stone Age. The remains are mainly Tudor and open to the public in the season. Around Laugharne, some of the common land, in the care of the unique Town Council, is still farmed in the mediaeval strip pattern.

The Route

The route of this walk follows roughly a figure-of-eight pattern, centred on the mainly Georgian town of Laugharne, and starts in the shadow of the castle on the sometimes-flooded foreshore. If the foreshore is flooded, the walk follows the main road south from the car park to-wards Pendine for about 400 metres before turning left up a narrow lane to Sir Johns Hill Farm, and then almost immediately left again down a short lane to a gate and stile on to a grassy track. Follow this track and pass a barn on your right. Here the track becomes a narrow sunken path down through trees to the foreshore (hopefully beyond any flooding). Turn right to continue the walk.

The main route – when the foreshore path is above water – follows the foreshore south from the car park, round the salt marsh until about 100 metres before a walled enclosure. A waymarked path by a bench climbs up into the trees.

1. Follow this path as it curves around the flanks of Sir Johns Hill, with views over the estuary and the marshes. At a waymarked fork in the paths, take the more worn option to the right, avoiding a descent to the marshes, and follow the path on until you come to a second fork by a ruin. Here a waymark points you north up a steep track.

2. At one point steep wooden steps have been provided. This track brings you to a stile into a field. Go straight on through a gateway in the hedge opposite and on, diagonally right across the field ahead, to a stile that comes out on a farm lane.

3. Turn left and follow the lane back towards the town.

4. At the end of the lane you have the choice of either following the 'flood route' right (described above), or the main road back to the start point.

   Back at the start you again have a choice of route depending on flood conditions. If the path is dry, cross the bridge and follow the foreshore under the castle and onwards until you come to a signpost pointing to Dylan Thomas's Boat House, just after a zigzag in the well-made, surfaced path. On reaching the lane at the top of the path, turn right. This route affords the finest views of the estuary and Boat House, but if it is flooded, follow the signposted route through town.

5. Both routes bring you to the blue-painted shed where Dylan Thomas wrote, and if you look through the window in the door you can see the restored interior – complete with rejected drafts crumpled on the floor and handy beer bottle!

   One hundred metres further on down steep steps is the Boat House, where Dylan Thomas lived, now having a tea shop, book shop and original furnishings, as well as a viewing platform.

6. After visiting the Boat House, regain the path and head northwards, right, following a wooded path above the estuary. Crossing a stile into a field, keep towards the right-hand hedge until you cross two stiles that bring you to the beautifully maintained Delacorse Farm.

7. Go through the farmyard and round the left of the house to gain the farm track that leads you back uphill towards the town. 35 metres past a turn-off to Brixtarw Farm, turn left up a surfaced lane signed 'unsuitable for wide vehicles', which then swings right down towards the church.

8. Enter the shady churchyard by a kissing gate on your right at its north end and, after visiting the church, cross the cobbled sunken lane by a bridge into the new section of the graveyard. Here Dylan Thomas's grave, marked by a plain white cross, is to be found. Leave this section of the graveyard by a kissing gate in the top hedge and turn right into a rough lane which zigzags back towards Laugharne. At a T-junction of tracks by some chalets, turn right into an ancient sunken lane that leads you back to a road into town.

Turn right on to this road and follow it as it bears right down to Market Street. Here either turn left to go back past the clock tower and castle to the start, or take a small diversion to the right and visit Browns Hotel. Here you can take a drink where Dylan Thomas drank (with memorabilia now on the walls) or even have a drink free from tobacco smoke in the non-smokers' bar, before returning to your vehicle.

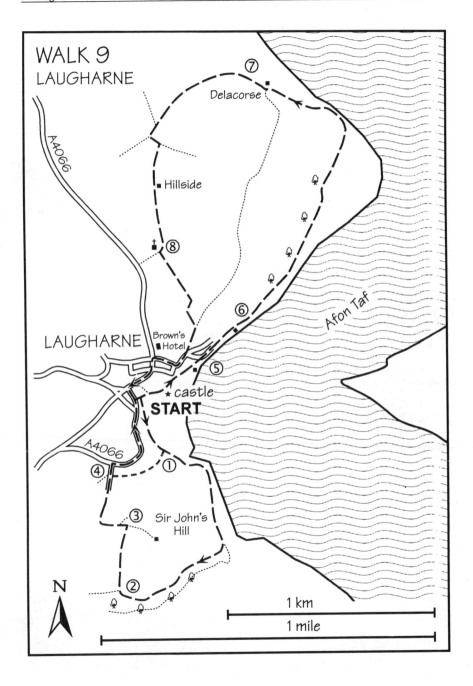

10: Llanboidy

Distance: 4½ miles (7.25km)

Time: 2½ hours

Maps: OS Pathfinder 1058 Llanboidy and Cynwyl Elfed, OS Landrangers 158 Tenby or 145 Cardigan and Surrounding Area.

Start: Car park and picnic site 218 231

Terrain: A mixture of paths and lanes. Can be muddy and overgrown in places.

Nearest Towns: Narberth and Carmarthen

Parking: See Start

Refreshments: Pubs and a shop in Llanboidy

Stiles: 10

Suitable for: All. Dogs on leads in farmland, please.

Along the way

Llanboidy was not always the quiet backwater it is today. On the contrary, it is the centre of a parish that was in the past very important with numerous remains left to indicate its status. There are prehistoric sites in the area, ranging from the Neolithic cromlech of Gwal-y-Filiast (Lair of Greyhound Bitch), through Bronze Age burial mounds, to the Iron Age hill fort at Hafod, which is passed during the walk.

A Roman road, the Via Julia, passed through the parish and Hafod hill fort appears to have been used as a Romano-British farm. Roman occupation of Hafod has been pretty well proven, and various Roman artefacts, including coins and a ring, have been found in the area.

After the Romans came the Irish-Celtic invasions, and burial stones bearing Ogham writing have been found near the village. Leg-

St Brynach's church, Llanboidy

end has it that St Brynach established the church here. Being re-
fused accommodation, he slept in a cowshed where he was visited
by an angel who told him to build a church where he saw a white
sow and her piglets. The next day he duly saw them and erected his
church, which was called Llanbeudy (the church of the cowshed).

Later the Normans appear to have taken the area from the Welsh
princes, building a motte and bailey castle in the south-west of the
village. When Whitland Abbey was built in the parish, the Cister-
cian monks came to own and farm large parts of the region. After the
Dissolution of the Monasteries, the land was taken over by private
landlords, with the Powell family of Maesgwynne Mansion having
the largest estate in Llanboidy.

From around 1565 the village prospered, its position on the drove
road from Newcastle Emlyn to St Clears definitely helping, with the
village providing 10 inns to help quench the drovers' thirst.

After about 1860 the fortunes of Llanboidy declined as the railway came to nearby St Clears and Whitland and drew trade away.
Some milling of both grain and cloth took place in the valley, but by
around 1930 this too had gone. A farmers' co-operative to produce

butter and cheese was opened opposite the church in 1880, but this closed quite quickly so little remains of Llanboidy's glory days.

However, the Maesgwynne Arms, built on the site of an old inn called The Farmers' Arms, still stands. Built in 1858 to house the visiting sporting friends of Squire Powell, who had previously built a local racecourse and was a keen fox-hunter, the Maesgwynne Arms was once attached by a covered bridge to The Oddfellows Lodge, where meetings of the Parish Vestry Brass Band and Shire Horse Society were held, as well as the local magistrates Sessions. When the Sessions moved to Whitland in 1905, the Lodge became a garage and then in 1907 was demolished.

Village life is now centred on the pubs, the church and the market hall. The market hall, paid for by the Squire's betting wins, was built in 1881 and included a coffee lounge and reading room, while the fountain outside reminds us that Llanboidy was the first village in Carmarthenshire to have a piped water and sewerage system. This was installed in 1890.

The church is dedicated to St Brynach, who founded this site in the fifth century. Some features of the early church remain with 18th and 19th-century additions. The original wooden bell tower has long gone and the present bell cote dates from the 1960s, replacing one built to commemorate the Battle of Waterloo. The church is well worth a visit, with beautiful stained glass windows and a marble statue of 'grief' on the Powell family vault.

The notable Scots pine in the churchyard is said to have been planted in the 18th century by Jacobite supporters, though others point to the traditional use of Scots pines as ley markers and claim the village lies on a major ley line.

Although this walk through the valley of the Afon Gronw includes quite a substantial proportion of road walking, these sections are on quiet, rural lanes with hedge banks full of wild flowers, including the rare Tenby daffodil, and are an attraction in their own right. The wildlife in the valley includes otters, foxes, herons, owls, woodpeckers, kingfishers, buzzards and much more. If you are very lucky, any, or all may be seen on this walk.

The Route

From the car park with its information board, cross the road and go through the gates opposite the car park entrance into the field that holds the remains of the motte and bailey castle.

1. Follow the left-hand hedge down to the corner where you will find a stile, a footbridge over a boggy section and a second footbridge over a stream. Cross these and follow the left-hand hedge through three more fields until you come to a gate into a large field.

   Cross this field on roughly the same line as the hedge behind you, passing a standing stone and heading for a prominent gap in the hedge line on the horizon. The standing stone is not marked on the map and it is unclear whether this is an ancient or modern stone, but its position could indicate the former.

   On the far side of the field you come to a stile and footbridge into a field below Parsonage Farmhouse. Follow the left-hand hedge round to a gate to the driveway. Go through the gate and turn right on the driveway up to a surfaced lane. Turn right and follow the lane down over the Afon Gronw, past Ddol Farm with its attractive pigs, and up to a T-junction. Turn right and keep on the lane down to Lower Llanboidy.

2. This part of Llanboidy grew up next to one of the old mills and by the bridge. Turn left at the junction to climb up above the valley on a wide, but quiet, lane. The views of the motte and bailey and Hafod hill fort are very good as you look north and west from the early part of this, the longest section of road walking.

   After approximately one mile, a little way after the attractive building of Haulfryn and opposite the not-so-attractive, modern Greenacres Manor, turn right down a narrow lane.

3. Some 100 metres down the lane, turn right through a gate into a field. Head almost due west across the field past an ancient oak, all that remains of what was one of the hedges of a green lane, down to a waymarked stile in the left-hand corner where fence and hedge meet.

   A faint path leads right to rejoin the sometimes wet and muddy, old sunken lane which you follow down through the trees to cross a footbridge over the Gronw at Cwm Factory. The industrial name for this sylvan spot comes from the woollen mill that once stood here. Traces of its ruins and those of the workers' cottages can still be seen and it is surprising to learn that some of the cottages were inhabited up until the mid 1930s.

4. Head up the valley on a broad track, which I understand was once the main Llanboidy to Whitland road, to Felin Isaf, an old grain mill by a ford over the Gronw. Pass between the buildings and the river and follow a good track up to a gate. Go through the gate to join part of the waymarked Landsker Borderlands Trail, taking the right-hand, lower fork. This leads you along the foot of the valley wall, over a footbridge and along under Hafod hill fort.

5. At the end of the track you go through a metal gate into the garden of a house, and along the side of Hafod Hill Pottery to gain the road. Turn left uphill and follow the road for approximately 500 metres to where the road turns sharp left.

Turn right here down a deeply sunken green lane, signed as a dead end and as 'unsuitable for motors', and follow it down to cross a stream. Here the lane gains a surface by the Llanboidy Sports and Social Club and Playing Fields, and is followed to enter the village opposite the church. Turn right past the chapel, the old milk factory, market hall and Maesgwynne Arms to regain the start of this short but pleasant walk.

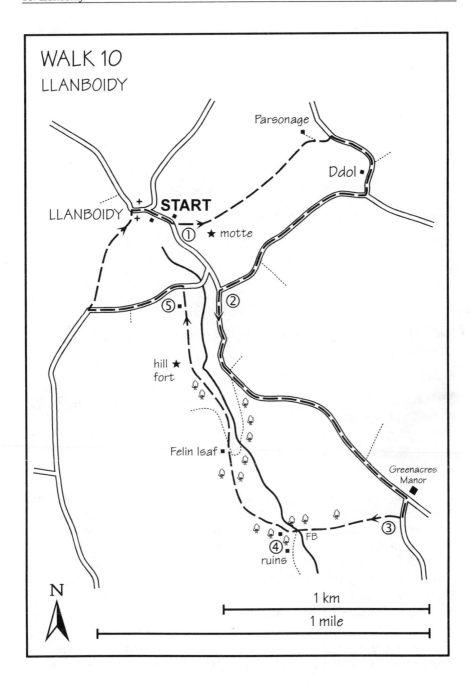

WALK 10
LLANBOIDY

Parsonage

Ddol

LLANBOIDY **START**

① ★ motte

②

⑤

hill ★
fort

Felin Isaf

Greenacres
Manor

③

FB

④
ruins

N

1 km

1 mile

11: Llanstephan

Distance: 5½ miles (8.75 km)

Time: 3 hours

Maps: OS Landranger 159 Swansea and The Gower, OS Pathfinders 1105 Pendine and 1081 St Clears and Laugharne.

Start: Castle end of foreshore parking in Llanstephan 353 105

Terrain: Mainly good field paths – muddy in places.

Nearest Town: Carmarthen

Parking: See Start

Public Transport: Limited bus service to Llanstephan village.

Refreshments: Shops, pubs and café in village, fish and chip caravan and café at the start.

Stiles: 12

Suitable for: All. Dogs may have difficulty with some stiles. Keep dogs on leads in farmland.

Along the way

Llanstephan is a quiet village on the estuary of the River Towy, brooded over by the ruins of its Norman Castle. Settlement on this site has been known from at least the Iron Age, the castle being built on an Iron Age promontory fort. Llanstephan reached the height of its popularity in the early part of the century as a holiday resort, mainly receiving miners from the Rhondda and railwaymen from Swindon. These visitors normally came by train to Ferryside, and then by ferry across the estuary.

The whole area is steeped in history and dominated by the castle. The ruins mainly date from the 15th century, but the castle was of stone construction from about 1200. Over the years it saw a lot of ac-

Llanstephan Castle

tion and rebuilding and seems to have changed hands – from Welsh to English ownership – many times in its bloody history.

After Owain Glyndwr's rebellion the castle's history became quieter and it was eventually abandoned. Now in the care of Cadw, the castle (once painted by Turner) is open to the public with no entrance fee and is well worth visiting. It commands superb views of the whole area including the Gower, the Towy estuary and the coast towards Pendine. No dogs are allowed. Leaflets on the castle are available from the post office in the village passed on the way.

Christianity over the years has left its mark on the area, and the walk passes the village church dedicated to the sixth-century Welsh Saint Ystyffan. This is an 11th-century building of immense charm built on a sixth-century site, huddled under the shoulder of the hills and is worth a visit. No dogs are allowed.

Also passed on this figure-of-eight route is St Anthony's Well, an ancient 'wishing well' (probably involved in pre-Christian rituals) which was adopted by a sixth-century hermit who called himself Anthony after the first-century St Anthony of Egypt. The hermit had great influence on the Celtic church in South Wales, using the waters in the well to baptise the pagan locals into the church. A place of pilgrimage, the well is supposed to have healing powers and be good for the lovelorn, who should leave a bent pin or coloured stone as an offering.

The Route

Leave the car park by the west (inland) corner and follow the path signed 'Castle' up to a surfaced lane. Turn right towards the village where guides to the castle (visited later in the walk) can be purchased in the post office opposite the church.

1. Cross the main road (!) and take the path that climbs out of the valley between the Sticks Hotel and the Castle Inn. This ancient, tree-lined lane brings you out into fields and, as you keep to the left-hand hedge, the route swings to the left, crossing several hedge lines by stiles and gates until joining a vehicle track to Llanfach. Here you follow the twin gravelled wheel lines left through a gate, and eventually to a quiet lane.

2. Cross the lane to a stile almost opposite which was not very well maintained at the time of writing, and head southwards down across the field, parallel to the right-hand hedge, to a gate and stile. Cross into the new field, follow the right-hand hedge and cross another stile and gate into another lane.

At the start of the track opposite, take the stile on your left into the field and follow the right-hand hedge to a stile in the corner. Note the superb views from this point. Go over this stile and follow the right-hand hedge halfway down the field to another awkward stile. Cross this and follow the left-hand hedge down to Parc Glas where a stile takes you onto their drive below the house and on to a rough track.

3. Parc Glas was formerly known as Tafarn Llaeth (the milk tavern) and specialised in serving milk fortified with spirits!

Turn right once past the house and take the track down towards the beach at Scotts Bay, taking the left of two gates you come to by a slate plaque reading 'Bwthyn Sant Antwn'. A short way past the

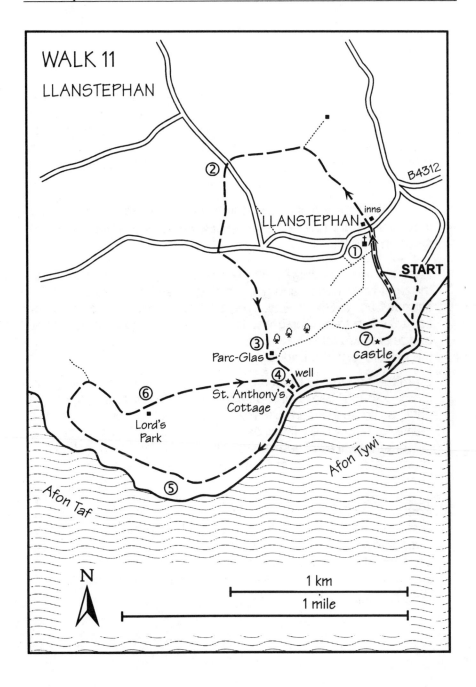

WALK 11
LLANSTEPHAN

② LLANSTEPHAN inns
B4312
① START
LLANSTEPHAN
② ③ Parc-Glas
⑦★ castle
④ well
⑥ St. Anthony's Cottage
Lord's Park
⑤
Afon Tywi
Afon Taf

N

1 km
1 mile

gate there is a door in the wall to your right with another plaque reading 'Ffynon Antwn Sant'. Go through to visit this charming holy well.

4. After trying your luck, making your wish or praying, rejoin the path to the beach and turn right over a bridge crossing an attractive stream. Take the partly wooded path ahead that gently climbs, crossing several stiles complete with 'dog gates', as it follows round the National Trust property of Lords Park, keeping above the low sandstone cliffs.

5. Round Wharley Point and eventually curl back inland to reach a lane. Turn right towards Lords Park Farm, signposted to Llanstephan Castle.

6. Pass the farm buildings to the left to join a footpath that keeps to the right-hand hedge and goes through a series of gates as it descends back to Scotts Bay. The last 100 metres or so of this section take in a tree-hung green lane, on the way down towards the bridge crossed earlier. Rejoining the coastal path, turn left through the gate to gain the bridge.

   From the bridge you have a choice: follow the beach – noting the many coloured bands of red sandstone in the cliffs on your left – until you come to a surfaced road that will lead you up towards the castle, or follow the clifftop path. After about half a mile, take the left fork that will also lead you towards the castle (the right fork descends steeply to the aforementioned road where it meets the beach).

7. Both options take you to the end of the public road leading to the castle. Turn left and climb the zigzag track and path up to the ruins. After enjoying the views and exploring the castle site, return to the car park either via the beach or by taking the road towards the village and retracing your earlier route down the signposted path and back to the start of the walk.

```
┌─────────────────────────────────────────────┐
│                                               │
│              12: Llandovery                   │
│                                               │
└─────────────────────────────────────────────┘
```

Distance: 8¼ miles (13km)

Time: 4 to 5 hours

Maps: OS Landranger 146 Lampeter and Llandovery, OS Pathfinder 1036 Llandovery.

Start: Car park by castle 767 342

Terrain: Mainly well-waymarked field paths and tracks. Muddy in places.

Nearest Town: Llandovery

Parking: See Start

Refreshments: Pubs, cafés, shops etc. in Llandovery

Stiles: 45, nearly all excellent

Suitable for: All. Dogs on leads in farmland, please.

Note: The path from near Pant y Gaseg to the junction with the green lane beyond the Round Lodge is a permissive path made available by the Forestry Commission. Please do nothing to jeopardise future access to this delightful route. The Information and Heritage Centre is open Monday to Saturday 10.00 to 13.00 and 13.45 to 16.00, Sunday 14.00 to 16.00.

Along the way

In his book *Wild Wales* George Borrow described Llandovery as 'about the pleasantest little town in which I have halted in the course of my wanderings', and the town still makes a good base for walks.

Surrounded by three rivers, the Bran, Gwydderig and the Towy, and by superb scenery, Llandovery has a long history and sits astride ancient trading routes through Wales. These routes from South-West Wales to Brecon and northwards, made Llandovery a strategic site, a point not missed by the Romans who built a fort on Llanfair Hill to the north of the town, near the junction of several of their famous roads.

The later motte and bailey castle on the south side of the town was first built between 1100 and 1116 by Richard Fitzponz, and was captured by the Welsh under Rhys of Deheubarth in 1162. The next century saw many changes of ownership amongst the Welsh, often hotly contested, but in 1277 the castle was given, peacefully, to the English crown and held under stewardship by John Giffard. It was this owner who built the castle which we see in ruins today. The castle reverted to the crown in 1490 and was held by Prince Arthur, the elder brother of Henry VIII, but was a ruin by the reign of Elizabeth I. Over the years much of the stone was recycled to build the grand houses of Llandovery, and all that now remains standing on the floodlit natural mound of the castle are fragments of the west end of the keep.

Being on important trading routes, Llandovery was an important centre for the drovers who moved livestock, notably Welsh Black cattle, from Welsh pastures to England. In 1799 David Jones, the drover, founded the Bank of the Black Ox in part of the King's Head Inn on the corner of Market Street and Stone Street, later moving to Prospect House in High Street, once a residence of the Bishop of St David's. The Bank flourished, even producing its own bank notes, and operated until 1909 when it merged with Lloyds Bank and the Black Ox became part of the Black Horse. The Llandovery branch of Lloyds is still located at Prospect House, while both the Heritage Centre and the Kings Head Inn have displays of the banking history of Llandovery.

Other famous residents of Llandovery include William Williams, the great hymn writer, and Twm Shon Catti, 'the Welsh Robin Hood'. In 1997 Llandovery College celebrated its 150th anniversary, and in 1996 the High School celebrated its centenary.

The drovers left a heritage not only of a bank, but also in the number of pubs and inns in the town – enough to slake any walker's thirst!

Part of the walk described here follows the Towy Valley and river bank, the river being one of the longest in Wales at some 70 miles. Its rich alluvial deposits support lush grasslands used in the county's dairy industry.

Round lodge at Llynywormwood Park near Llandovery

Some of the route passes through the remains of Llynyworm-wood Park, once part of a large estate. Llynywormwood House was built in the early 19th century by the Williams family, later Griffies-Williams, baronets, and was a focal point of the local social scene. Set in a superb spot with views of the Carmarthen Fans and with parkland and ancient woodland, the house must have been a delight, but the estate was broken up in 1910, the house becoming a girls' school until 1939, and now sadly a ruin. The woods were taken over by the Forestry Commission and replanted with conifers, though much of the broadleaf woodland remains. In the woods you will come across a fine stone bridge dated 1812, and the strangely named Round Lodge. It is, in fact, octagonal.

The walk offers a variety of scenery with some excellent views, while the wildlife is plentiful and varied. Look out for an enormous selection of wild flowers from campions to purslane, vetches to foxgloves, and numerous birds such as goldcrests, buzzards and, if you are lucky, a red kite or two, and even kingfishers and dippers on the streams. Mammals in the area include foxes, rabbits, grey squirrels and badgers.

The Route

Leave the car park by the entrance opposite the castle ruins, past the Information and Heritage Centre and by the statue of a drover, turning right onto King's Road. Cross at the pelican crossing and turn left at the junction with Stone Street, where you find the excellent Dinefwr Craft Centre. Continue up Stone Street, the mediaeval way into Llandovery, past the King's Head Inn and the Bank of the Black Ox, up the No Entry section to a crossroads. Go straight over, up Cilycwm Road – signed to Cilycwm and Rhandir-Mwyn – past the school and under the railway bridge.

1. Some 300 metres beyond the railway, leave the road for a way-marked footpath over a stile to your right by a wooden bench. You soon come to a footbridge over an embanked stream, which is followed for some 500 metres. Recross the stream then almost immediately take another footbridge left, into an open field.

    Follow the right-hand hedge up to a gateway by a 'private' pond, where you turn left, following along the fence to gain a track into coppiced oak woodland in the corner. Do not drop down left to the fields, but follow this excellent track almost as far as Dolauhirion. Take the stile to your left just above the farm and drop down across the field to the stile opposite and on to the road.

2. Turn left, then right towards the ancient and very attractive Pont Dolauhirion Bridge with its attendant waterfall, but do not cross the bridge. Take the stile left just before the bridge and follow the river bank for some 600 metres.

    As you come parallel with the buildings of Manorafon, the path bears left up the field to a stile some 100 metres in from the river and crosses into a hedged lane by a stream. From the end of the lane the path goes right over a footbridge and is clearly guided round the north and west of Tonn Farm and across their drive to follow a fence line down to some sheds.

3. Here you gain a track, initially hedged both sides, then only on the left, which leads you down to the A40 by the Chain Bridge. Turn right but do not cross the bridge, crossing just before it to a stile which leads you back to the riverside path.

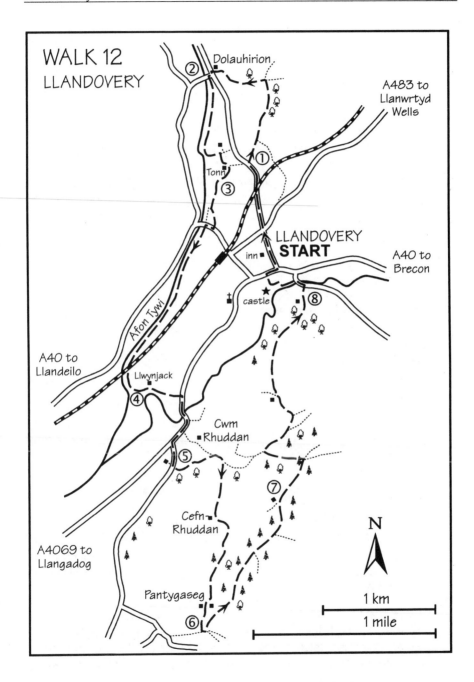

WALK 12
LLANDOVERY

Dolauhirion

A483 to
Llanwrtyd
Wells

Tonn

LLANDOVERY
START

A40 to
Brecon

inn

castle

A40 to
Llandeilo

Afon Tywi

Llwynjack

Cwm
Rhuddan

A4069 to
Llangadog

Cefn
Rhuddan

Pantygaseg

N

1 km

1 mile

The river path between sports grounds, Llandovery RFC pitch, a golf course and the river is followed for just over a mile, passing under a low railway bridge (not a place to be when a train is overhead). Just beyond some piles of gravel and shingle, the river is abandoned for a track up past Llwynjac.

4. The path bears right off the track before you enter the yard and crosses a field before rejoining the farm drive and following this up to the A4069. Turn right on the road and follow it for approximately 500 metres, over the bridge over the river to a T-junction. Turn left up the road signed to Myddfai (note the old milestone by the letter box) and climb up to a track that joins the road opposite Penroc Cottage.

5. Turn left up the track and follow it left under the wooded hill as views open up over the Towy Valley and Llandovery. Coming to a fork in the track after about 500 metres, bear right. Next drop off the track to a stile in the field boundary, to the left of a gate signed 'Cefn Rhuddan Farm'. Follow the right-hand hedge up to a stile to the farm track, which you then follow uphill. The path crosses into the field on the left to avoid the farmyard, but regains the track just beyond the buildings, heading west-south-west.

    At a fork in the track bear right through a gate and uphill. Follow the track as it swings right and down towards a felled area of conifers, where it goes left to an obscured stile then right again between some broadleaf woods and the felled conifers. Coming out into fields, follow the left hedge to a gate and stile. Cross the hedge and keep it on your right as you head for Pantygaseg Farm.

6. Go through the farmyard and down the farm drive to a junction of tracks. Turn left and follow a permissive path along the track (ignore the path to the right near the track junction) and into the woods. Note the old bridge in the trees on your right some 500 metres into the woods.

    Where the track leaves the woods for a field, leave the track and follow a path up left through the fringes of the wood, eventually regaining the track some 250 metres further on. If you look right along this section, you have the most superb view up the valley of the Afon Ydw, past the ruins of Llynywormwood House to the Carmarthen Fans.

Turn left on regaining the track and follow it for some 600 metres past the Round Lodge to a cross track junction with a green lane.

7. Turn left through a gate and stile and follow the track down through the woods and across a boggy meadow to a track junction, where you turn right up to a gate. From the gate bear left, north-north-east, uphill, following the left fence to a gateway that gives superb views over Llandovery to the 'green desert' of Mid Wales.

Follow the track you join north-west and north down through Cefn-yr-Allt-Uchaf farmyard, then enter a field by the derelict farmhouse. Follow the right-hand hedge to a gate and stile into the next field, which is crossed diagonally to the far corner.

Again, cross the next field diagonally right down to a stile into woods in the far bottom corner. Bear right, north-east, down the track through the woods to a fork at the bottom of the woods, where you bear right on the higher path along to a stile into a field.

8. Turn left and descend through Bronallt Farm to the road, where you turn left and cross the river by Waterloo Bridge. At the end of the bridge, drop left down some steps to gain a riverside walk which leads you directly back to the Castle Mound and the start of the walk. I recommend that time is spent in the Heritage Centre and in exploring the town.

13: Mynydd Mallaen

Distance: 11 miles (18 km)

Time: 7 hours

Maps: OS Landranger 147 Elan Valley and Builth Wells, OS Pathfinder 1013 Cilycwm and Pumsaint. The Pathfinder is recommended as the navigation through farmland is difficult and this map shows the field boundaries.

Start: Roadside at 753 407

Terrain: A mix of rough upland, moors and field paths. Muddy or boggy in places. The path can be indistinct in places.

Nearest Town: Llandovery

Parking: Limited roadside parking near the start. Do not obstruct gates or traffic.

Refreshments: None but streams

Stiles: 8

Suitable for: Those with experience in hillwalking and map and compass work. Bad weather can blow in quickly and the top of the mountain is featureless, making it easy to get lost if hill fog, cloud, rain etc. set in.

Note: Full hillwalking kit and boots, waterproofs, spare clothing, spare food, first aid kit, compass, whistle and survival bag are all needed. This is a serious and committing walk, though highly enjoyable! Many stiles are missing, but the barbed wire has been removed at most fence crossings.

Along the way

Although modern walkers should take along every modern aid to comfort and safety, these hills have been walked by man since before civilisation dawned. The route takes in two standing stones

The track up Rhiw Cilgwyn

from prehistoric times: Maen Bach, and a larger one, just noted as a 'standing stone' on the map. Both insignificant close to, these stones are carefully sited to dominate a large area and be seen from afar.

Other early remains nearby include: the course of a Roman aqueduct servicing their gold mine at Dolaucothi, cairns at various points, remains of mines and quarries in the cwms, and the old road from Cilycwm to Cwrt y Cadno that forms the first part of the route described.

The Route

Leave the road, taking the farm drive up to Glangwenlais Farm. Follow the waymarks through the farmyard, diagonally across the front of the house, through a gate and down to a stile by a stream and some gardens. Cross the stream by a footbridge and then turn right through the farmyard of Penstacan to follow a broad path up the cwm and past woods for about 200 metres beyond the buildings of Penstacan.

1. Here, at a track junction, go straight ahead through a gate and up a stream-encroached track along the left of the field for 200 metres.

Go past a pond built on the ancient track to a corner, then turn right uphill with the hedge on your left. Continue straight on up the hill as the faint path develops into a rough track, the old road to Cwrt y Cadno. In places you can make out ruts worn into the rock by the cartwheels.

After traversing above a forestry plantation in Cwm Merchon, the track comes to a saddle between two hills and bears left and up – now a well-graded roadway – swinging onto the south flank of Rhiw Cilgwyn above Nant Fran as it climbs up on to the plateau above.

2. The track on the plateau is obvious (especially after it is joined by a track coming up from the forestry to the south, though is less distinct again after a crossroads of tracks between the fords). It is easy to follow it as it crosses this desolate area (ignore tracks turning off to the left and right) and takes you over two fords.

3. The first ford, Rhyd Galed, is easy to cross.

4. Crossing the second, Rhydd Ddu, is more difficult. It is very boggy and after rain can pose problems in crossing dry-shod. About 500 metres beyond Rhyd Ddu, the track brings you to a path junction by the gate in the fence that has been visible on your left for some time.

5. Here the good path is abandoned and the faint, and in places intermittent, track heading north-east over Pen Cerrigdiddos is followed. The right of way does not follow the obvious path that follows the eastern flank of the hill, but the less obvious path that holds more to the west of the high ground. Both paths meet up nearer Maen Bach. Note the stone slabs along the start of this section: some believe these to be ancient standing stones now toppled.

Avoiding as much bog as possible, the intermittent path keeps bearing roughly north-east along the high ground between the Nant Dan and the Afon Gwenlais before swinging around the headwaters of the latter, heading more easterly, making for Maen Bach.

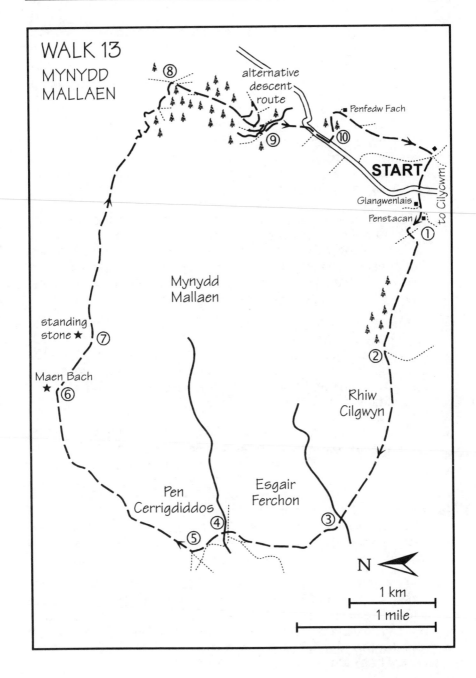

WALK 13
MYNYDD
MALLAEN

(8)
alternative
descent
route

Penfedw Fach

(9)
(10)

START

Glangwenlais
Penstacan
(1)

to Cilycwm

Mynydd
Mallaen

standing
stone ★
(7)

Maen Bach
★
(6)

(2)

Rhiw
Cilgwyn

Pen
Cerrigdiddos
(4)
(5)

Esgair
Ferchon

(3)

N

1 km

1 mile

6. This standing stone is not on the right of way according to the map, but the faint track leads to it and makes the ancient marker an obvious point to aim for. From Maen Bach the magnificent views include the next prehistoric waymark on the route, the standing stone to the south-east.

7. Here the track starts to become more obvious and is easily followed, becoming quite steep and rocky as it descends towards the forestry plantations of Cwm y Rhaiadr. Continue for approximately 600 metres down from the top of these woods, to where the edge of the plantation bends from south-east to south-south-west.

8. Here, by some old, tree-covered sheepfolds, leave the main path just before it goes down through the third gate since leaving the open hill. Follow the path on your right down through the trees. This section can be a little confusing but, by close attention to the map and with an eye out for waymarks, the path, faint in places, brings you to a footbridge over the Nant y Rhaiadr.

   Alternatively, zigzag down the forestry tracks, as shown on the map. First turn left as you join the first major forestry track, then right, signed 'Campsite', at the next junction. At the third track junction (ignoring minor paths) go left then, after you meet a path coming in from the left, you go down right, through a hunters' gate, to reach the bridge.

9. Cross over the footbridge and turn left on to an often muddy track that soon leaves the stream and crosses farmland to reach the road. Turn right and follow the road for about 300 metres, then turn left up the farm track towards Penfedw Fach.

10. Just before the farmhouse, turn right through a gate into fields and follow the hedge on your right. After approximately 500 metres, near the top of the hill, you cross a stile and follow the hedge on your left. Follow this for about 750 metres, through several fields.

   You will reach a gate and a major track/path junction by the corners of a number of fields near Caer Beili. Here you cross into the field ahead and turn right (north-west) across this boggy field, aiming for the far corner. Cross into the next field and follow the boundary on your right down to cross a stile, then a stream to join a muddy track to regain the start of the walk.

14: Nant y Ffin

Distance: 6½ miles (10 km)

Time: 4 hours

Maps: OS Landranger 146 Lampeter and Llandovery, OS Pathfinder 1035 Pencader.

Start: Forestry picnic site 544 315

Terrain: Forest tracks, paths and old green lane. Muddy in places. One ford difficult when river in spate.

Nearest Town: Lampeter and Carmarthen

Parking: See Start

Refreshments: None on the route, though good pub in nearby Brechfa.

Public Transport: None

Stiles: None

Suitable for: All. Dogs on leads in farmland.

Along the way

Most of this walk is on forestry paths and tracks. However, this does not mean that the walk passes through serried ranks of dark conifers as broadleaf woods dominate. Brechfa Forest has always been a woodland area and although much of the forest is now coniferous, the original ash and oak woods were once important mediaeval hunting grounds. Much wood was harvested in the early 20th century to fuel the industries of South Wales. During the First World War the local timber was used to make naphtha for explosives.

Although timber production still goes on, the forest now supports many leisure activities with waymarked walking and cycle routes laid out, as well as intrusive sports such as the RAC Rally which holds stages in the forest. Despite this, the woods are generally quiet and home to a great range of wildlife. Look out for red kites, red

squirrels, gold-crests, nuthatches and kingfishers. Lichens and mosses, ferns and bilberries thrive here, as do various mammals such as foxes and badgers.

The Route

From the picnic site follow the forestry track up between oak and silver birch – note the waymarks and 'walker welcome here' signs – keeping to the well-graded surface for approximately 600 metres. You then cross a stream and come to a T-junction of broad tracks.

In the woods, near Nant y Ffin

1. Ignore left and right turns and follow a narrow, waymarked path straight on, zigzagging up through a majestic stand of 60-year-old Douglas firs, and on through stands of young conifers and coppiced oak. Ignore any cross paths and stay on the intermittently waymarked path.

Passing through areas of mature oak and beech, you come to a field edge before the path drops back down to meet a wide forestry track. Turn left and follow this track for approximately 200 metres to a corner. Here the waymarked path cuts off right and, still swinging right, descends to a broad forestry track by the side of the Nant-y-Ffin stream.

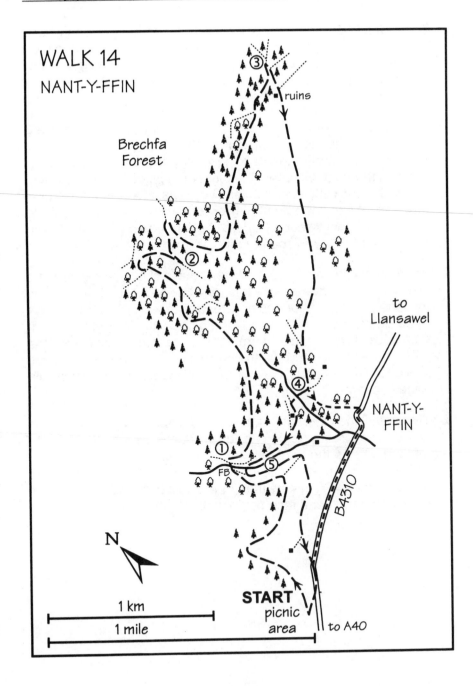

2. Turn left and follow the track over a bridge to a T-junction where the route goes right up the main path and climbs upward to give superb views of the Cothi Valley. At the top of the climb ignore the waymarked turn to the left and go straight on to a major path junction some 300 metres further on.

3. Turn hard right, almost doubling back on yourself, on to an ancient green lane. This leads you out of the trees past the ruins of Rhandir-gini, an old farm building where 'travellers' have set up camp in the past. Go down the often muddy, often rugged track, with its bedrock showing in extensive areas, to a lane/track crossroads some one and a quarter miles further on. The first part of this descent is down through fields and offers views of the charming valley below, but you soon regain the shelter of the trees.

4. From the track/lane crossroads you have a choice. If the streams are in spate you can avoid a tricky ford by going straight on down the lane to the road, turning right for a road walk of approximately three-quarters of a mile back to the picnic site. Alternatively, turn right down a rather water-worn track to the ford. Once across the ford – hopefully dry-shod – the ancient track is followed until you turn off left on a narrow, waymarked path some 250 metres past a ruined cottage.

5. This path winds through the trees and across another stream to join a broad forestry track. Turn left and follow this, ignoring a waymarked path to the right just after the track turns right, as it becomes a surfaced lane that leads you down to the road approximately 200 metres from the access to the picnic site. Turn right on the road and right again up the track back to the start.

15: Pembrey

Distance: 5 miles (8 km)

Time: 3 hours

Maps: OS Landranger 159 Swansea and Gower, OS Pathfinder 1106 Llanelli (North) and OS Explorer 10 Gower.

Start: Picnic site 419 013

Terrain: Mainly good paths through woodland, fen and farmland. Some road walking.

Nearest Town: Burry Port

Parking: See Start

Refreshments: one shop passed on the route.

Public Transport: Pembrey is on a regular bus route. Telephone SWT on Swansea (01792) 580580 for details.

Stiles: 14

Suitable for: All. Dogs on leads in Nature Reserves and farm land, please.

*The section between Penybedd Wood and the rail crossing at Peny-
bedd is on a permissive path courtesy of T. and F.E. Davies. Please do
nothing to jeopardise the future use of this path.*

Along the way

The diversity of scenery covered in this walk is immense as it passes
through woodland, fen and farmland. The first wood passed
through is Penybedd Wood, part of Pembrey Forest, which is mainly
coniferous and managed as a Forest Nature Reserve by Forestry Enterprise. Further on is Coed Rhyal, a mainly sessile oak wood showing coppice regrowth, managed by Dyfed Wildlife Trust. Coed Rhyal

is a magnificent sight in early summer with drifts of bluebells carpeting the ground.

Ffrwd Fen Nature Reserve, also passed on the route, is one of the few freshwater marshes left in the area, and is an SSSI managed by Dyfed Wildlife Trust. Here there are many rare plants including marsh pea and frogbit, as well as reed beds and willows.

The views from the walk are extensive, across the flat land of the Gwendraeth Valley to the Gower and Worms Head, and over the massed conifers of Pembrey Forest and Country Park to Cefn Sidan Sands. These sands have proved the final resting place of many ships, some by mishap, others, it is said, lured to their doom deliberately to provide plunder for the wreckers known as 'Gwyr-y-Bwelli Bach' or 'The Men of Little Hatchets'. They were named after the locally made tool, a hatchet incorporating a claw for ripping open cargo and equally useful for dispatching unwanted witnesses to the wreckers' activities.

In 1828 one victim of the sands was the ship 'La Jeune Emma', bound from the West Indies to France and blown badly off course. Thirteen of the 19 on board drowned, including Adeline Coquine, the 12-year-old niece of Napoleon Bonaparte's divorced wife, Josephine de Beauharnais. The survivors had a poor time of it amongst the lawless locals, but Adeline received a decent burial in Pembrey Church.

The church itself, dedicated to St Illtud, is a fascinating building. It was founded in 1066-1075 and seems to have grown and grown. Unfortunately, the church appears to be kept locked, but even a stroll around it shows the several different stages of construction, seemingly based on a simple bellcote style church but now including a striking tower and some attractive stained glass.

The whole area has a fascinating history and, although now predominantly rural in character, once hummed with heavy industry: with mining and coal extraction from open seams on Pembrey Mountain; the Royal Ordnance Factory, where now the Country Park thrives; and railways to serve them all. Little is now to be seen except for one old mine shaft passed in Coed Rhyal, the remains of the old mineral railway trackbed and the choked waters of the old canal by Ffrwd Fen.

Hidden from sight in Court Wood above the walk is an ancient hill fort, while ivy cloaks most of the mainly Elizabethan manor of

Penybedd Wood

Pembrey Court. This was originally built in 1128 though it was much altered in later years and is now a ruined shell that is easy to miss as you walk by. The once busy Spitfire airfield is now the Motor Sports Centre with buzzards, kestrels and marsh harriers ruling the air. While the paths that link forest and fen show the scars of past industry, nature shows its healing power by covering old workings in a cloak of wild flowers.

The Route

From the car park in the picnic site, follow the path along the fence on the left side of the woods. This sandy track soon winds its way into the trees, where there is more birdsong than you might expect from a coniferous forest. After following blue waymark posts for some 800 metres, you reach a T-junction of paths, where you turn right. Follow the broad track through the woods for approximately 300 metres to a crossroads of tracks and turn left. The track swings left, then right and leaves the woods past a forestry office and a former forestry worker's cottage, now privately owned and extended.

1. The track then zigzags through farmland, where a golf course is planned, past some cottages and parallel to the main line railway from Fishguard to London. At Penybedd turn right at a track crossroads and cross over the level crossing and main road to take a quiet lane towards Ffrwd Fen.

2. After crossing the bed of the dismantled mineral railway, take the path alongside the old canal and the Nature Reserve, signposted 'Llwybr St Illtud Walk' and 'Mountain Walks' up to the B4317. Cross the road to take the track opposite, but where the track swings left towards a private house, take the path signposted 'Mountain Walks' up to a stile into the woods.

3. Once over the stile, turn left, signed 'St Illtud Walk' and follow the edge of the woods, where bluebells and honeysuckle are rampant in their season.

   At a T-junction of paths, both signed 'Mountain Walks', turn left and descend above the house, following the lower edge of the

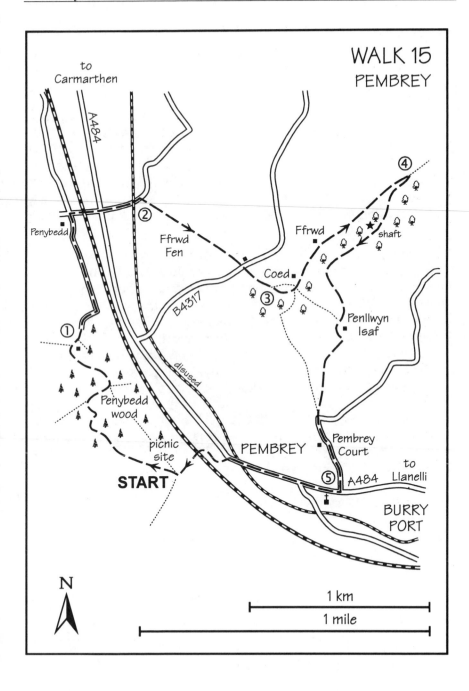

WALK 15
PEMBREY

to
Carmarthen

A484

Penybedd

②

Ffrwd
Fen

B4317

Ffrwd

Coed

④

shaft

③

Penllwyn
Isaf

①

disused

Penybedd
wood

picnic
site

START

PEMBREY

Pembrey
Court

⑤

A484

to
Llanelli

BURRY
PORT

N

1 km

1 mile

wood along to a farm lane. Turn right, again signed 'Mountain Walks', and follow the lane, with its extensive views over the valley, for some 650 metres, below Coed Rhydal, to a grassy track coming down from the right.

4. Go up this track, almost doubling back on yourself, over a metal stile and up to a waymark post. Here you leave the track on a narrow path going right. Follow this as it initially hugs the top of the trees, then climbs up over a waymarked stile, then goes on and up steps through woods to a T-junction of paths. Turn right and over a stile to come out at the top of the woodland, past an old mine shaft, before dropping right to follow the path along the top of the steep slopes of Coed Rhyal.

   Eventually, the path leads you out into a field. Bear left, keeping to the top of the slope with the boundary on your left until you come to a corner. From the point of the corner drop down right, signposted 'Mountain Walks', to a stile directly below in the far hedge. Cross this stile, turn left and follow the hedge round the field to another stile. Cross this and turn right, following the right-hand hedge down several fields until after about 500 metres you come out at a lane. Follow the lane straight on downhill, passing the ruins of Pembrey Court, through a housing estate to the main road.

5. Cross the road and turn right through Pembrey, past the fascinating church and on over the bridge across the old mineral railway to the junction signed 'Country Park'. Turn left, cross the main line railway and follow the lane back to the start of the walk at the picnic site.

16: Pendine

Distance: 7 miles (11 km)

Time: 4 to 5 hours

Maps: OS Pathfinder 1105 Pendine, OS Landranger 158 Tenby.

Start: Car park by Museum of Speed 236 080

Terrain: Mainly good, well-waymarked paths. Several very steep climbs.

Nearest Towns: Tenby, Carmarthen

Parking: See Start, or car park on the beach – note the tides well before leaving your car on the sands!

Refreshments: Many and varied in Pendine during season.

Stiles: 6

Suitable for: Those who can manage sustained steep ascents. Dogs on leads on farmland, please.

Along the way

Pendine is probably most famous for its sands, which run for approximately five miles to join Laugharne Sands and the Taf Estuary. At low tide the beach is almost half a mile wide and is backed by the wide sand dunes of Pendine Burrows. Although the sands are very popular with holidaymakers, most of the beach and sands are controlled by the Ministry of Defence, and are a 'Danger Area' as part of a weapons-testing area. However, by the village, part of this expanse of beach is always open to the public and when the red flags are not flying, so is the rest of the beach.

In the past this massive, flat beach has been the scene of much excitement, with the world land speed record being challenged and broken here many times by such luminaries as Sir Malcolm Campbell, Guilio Foresti and Parry Thomas. A sign on the wall of the Beach Hotel, headquarters of many an attempt on the land speed

Churchyard cross, Marros

record, lists the major achievements by the speed kings, and if you are interested in history and speed, the Museum of Speed, situated by the start of the walk, will be an added attraction.

Man has inhabited this area a lot longer than cars have been around and the walk passes many sites of prehistoric and historic interest including the ancient fortified settlement and possible stone circle on Gilman Point, chambered cairns above Morfa Bychan and an ancient settlement on the flanks of Marros Mountain. More recent historically interesting sights are to be found in the ruins of Marros Mill on the beach at Marros Sands, the ruined lime kilns and abandoned quarries in the woods below Marros Mountain and the churches at Marros and Pendine.

St Lawrence's Church in Marros has a massive 70ft tower, added to the church in the 13th or 14th century for defence (or prestige), which once housed the village school, while the church itself is probably based on a Celtic site. Note the initials carved in the church wall – not gratuitous graffiti, but showing which parishioners were responsible for each section's maintenance. The remains of an ancient cross are to be seen near the church porch, and by the road there is a most unusual war memorial styled on the chambered cairns at nearby Ragwen Point.

St Margaret's Church, Pendine has a 'saddle back' tower with unusual, slated, pitched roof. This is a 16th-century addition to a church which was probably founded by St Teilo in the sixth century. There is the stump of the old cross in the churchyard and a fascinating cast iron gravestone nearby. Both churches boast some interesting stained glass windows and have the peaceful atmosphere only found in churches of immense age.

The predominantly limestone geology of the area adds some interesting features to the walk, mainly stunning cave-riddled cliff scenery and views that stretch from Worms Head to Caldy Island and, on good days, Devon. Marros Beach, as well as having interesting natural stone 'platforms' on the beach, can also reveal the rare sight of a submerged forest which stretches hundreds of metres out to sea, showing the trunks and branches and peaty floor of a forest that was lost to the sea thousands of years ago.

At the Green Bridge, where the walk crosses the road to Amroth for the second time, the stream disappears under the natural limestone bridge the road is built on, but does not reappear on the other side. It is swallowed into the cave-riddled rocks below the dry valley on the far side of the road, not to reappear until it reaches Morfa Bychan a mile away. Only surface run-off water in modern concrete channels is found on the surface of the valley.

The wild flowers of the area reflect the limestone base of the land and are to be found in great profusion. Foxgloves, oxeye daisies, scarlet pimpernel, flag iris, ransoms, bluebells, foxgloves, stonecrop and many others can be seen, and there is evidence of a varied mammalian population. The variety of wildlife and superb views give ample opportunity for stops to look at the view on this rather strenuous but not overlong walk.

The Route

From the car park, follow the track past the Museum of Speed and toilets and down the slipway to the beach. Turn right and follow the beach to its western end then go up the steps on to the cliff path, waymarked 'The Carmarthen Bay Coastal Path'. If the beach is covered by the sea, follow the road from the car park, then by the Spring-Well Inn and snack bar to gain the cliff path. The initial climb is steep, narrow and, in places, slippery, and the ascent of some 85 metres seems to go on for ever, but a convenient bench at the top allows you to regain your breath in comfort. Continuing along the more level clifftop path, take the left fork under the ancient settlement on Gilman Point then zigzag left, then right to descend to Morfa Bychan.

1. The path crosses the track to the beach (note the vandalised stiles and waymark post) before passing below a huge concrete wall of seemingly Second World War vintage to climb an obvious (and steep) zigzag path back up under the shadow of the chambered cairns to the cliff top again.

    Passing through a kissing gate, turn left on to a track which is followed for about 175 metres to a fork in the track with a waymark post. Take the left fork and gentle descent to Marros Sands, guided by frequent waymark posts. In places where streams have colonised the path the going can be quite muddy even in dry weather.

2. The path follows the shingle banks backing Marros Sands with the sea on your left. Reed beds and willows thriving in the narrow strip of land between the shingle and hill behind form a lush 'jungle', contrasting with the beach 'desert'.

    Just past the ruins of Marros Mill, where the stream can be heard rushing through the shingle under your feet, turn right at a waymarked post and follow the path inland to join the track that serves the cottages by the mill. Turn left and follow this track up under limestone cliffs, ignoring the waymarked turn left to 'Underhill' and the Carmarthen Bay Coastal Path at the track junction after a gate and kissing gate. Instead of turning left here go right and follow the intermittently surfaced lane to the church, unusual war memorial and road at Marros.

3. Cross the road and take the track opposite with 'Honey Cottage' on the gate and follow this down across Marros Mountain. The right of way actually diverges from the track, but at present appears totally overgrown and impassable, but track and right of way join again by the cottage at the bottom of the track. If you can find the right of way, use it. If not, follow the track. At the bottom of the slope, right of way and track rejoin at a fork with 'Honey Cottage' signed to the left. Go right here, past a cottage and through an iron gate by a ruined cottage, on to a track at the bottom of a wood.

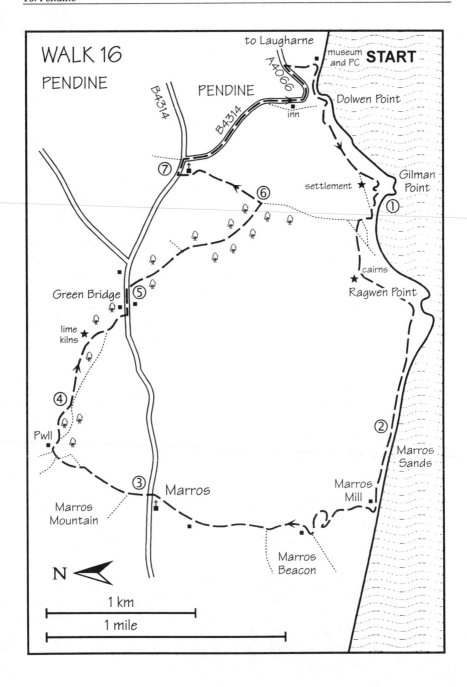

WALK 16
PENDINE

to Laugharne

A4066

museum and PC **START**

Dolwen Point

B4314

PENDINE

B4314

inn

⑦

settlement ★

Gilman Point

①

cairns

Ragwen Point ★

Green Bridge ⑤

⑥

lime kilns ★

④

Pwll

②

Marros Sands

③ Marros

Marros Mill

Marros Mountain

Marros Beacon

N

1 km

1 mile

4. Follow the left-hand boundary for some 200 metres, noting the Tolkienesque qualities of the wooded, and at one time quarried, slopes to your right. Coming out of the woods, you climb diagonally right across a field to a gap in the hedge ahead. Cross above a small wood, drop slightly below some more trees, cross into another field (with only partial hedges), then follow the right-hand boundary as it leads you down to a gateway gap on to an obvious track in the woods again.

The path to the woods is not obvious on the ground and care is needed to follow the right of way along this section. Try and keep the stream below in sight, keep one eye on the map and one on the compass and you should be fine. Once in the woods, follow the obvious track bearing right past some old lime kilns up to a field. Bear left, following the top of the woods, on to a gated track which is then followed southwards to a road. Turn left past Green Bridge Farm, noting its unusual tile roof and round chimneys, and go down to the Green Bridge in the dip.

5. Turn right down a waymarked track here and follow this down the valley for approximately three-quarters of a mile.

6. On a bend with a vandalised waymark, take the path left and climb gently up a wooded stream valley on an excellent path between fields to join the B4314. On reaching the road turn left, then almost immediately leave it again, turning left up a track signed as a no through road, up to the church.

7. Go through the churchyard then turn right to regain the B4314. Turn right and follow the road past Great House Farm, an ancient and architecturally interesting, if run-down, building. The gateway has front pillars surmounted by huge balls which were originally at the entrance to old Tremoilet Mansion.

The road leads steeply down – note the escape lane on the road – to the right-angle bend by the Spring-Well Inn. A plaque on the sea wall tells how a bus driver 'gave his life to save others', presumably after suffering brake failure before the escape lane was built! Turn left along the road past the Beach Hotel, or along the beach to regain the start of the walk.

17: Rhandirmwyn

Distance: 8¼ miles (13km)

Time: 4 to 5 hours

Maps: OS Landranger 160 Breacon Beacons or 146 Lampeter and Llandovery, OS Pathfinders 1013 Cilycwm and Pumsaint and 1036 Llandovery.

Start: Rhandirmwyn 784 437

Terrain: Field paths and tracks, forestry tracks and quiet lanes. Muddy in places. Indistinct in places.

Nearest town: Llandovery

Parking: Limited roadside parking at start.

Refreshments: The Royal Oak Inn and PO shop, Rhandirmwyn.

Stiles: 17, most excellent. Some gates will not open and need climbing over.

Suitable for: All. Dogs on leads in farmland, please.

Along the way

Although Rhandirmwyn is now a quiet little straggle of houses set in the beautiful upper Towy Valley, a spot so quiet that it holds a gem of a Christian Retreat Centre, life here was not always so peaceful and tranquil. The hills behind the village are covered with dense conifer forest, a modern development that will not be to everyone's taste, and this cloaks extensive remains of a once-thriving lead mining operation.

Although lead may have been mined here by the Romans, and perhaps even earlier, the main era of mining was in the 1770s, finally ceasing in the 1930s. The Nant y Bai mine was once the biggest mine in Carmarthenshire, if not South Wales, producing at one time as much as 4000 tonnes of lead per year. Some levels were perma-

Old track into the woods near Rhandirmwyn

nently flooded and workers traversed them by boat to reach dry workings on the far side. Surprisingly, the mine never seems to have been served by any tram or rail system, though it does appear to have had a water-wheel and later a steam-powered crushing mill. All the ore went first to Carmarthen and later to Llanelli in donkey-carried panniers, and then on by lorry.

Coming across the signs of mining in this secluded valley is a bit of a surprise these days, but is interesting from an industrial archaeological point of view. Many remains are visible from the walk described, though exploration should not include the entering of any shafts or adits as this can be extremely dangerous. Some fine examples of lead ore and interesting crystals can still be found on the spoil tips by the walk and behind the campsite near the village.

These days the main industries in the area are farming and forestry, with many tourists finding the scenery superb for walking, where not totally shrouded in monoculture coniferous planting. It is no coincidence that the valley from Rhandirmwyn to Llyn Brianne holds several well-frequented campsites for visitors to use as bases for exploring the area. It was to preserve the beauty of the Towy Valley that a campaign was launched when SWALEC wanted to raise a line of power cables from the hydroelectric scheme at Llyn Brianne all the way to Llandovery. The Blaenau Tywi Defence Committee, an assembly of local people, took on the mighty electricity company and eventually forced them to lay the cables underground and out of sight. Victory for the people, the scenery and sense!

The wide valley, flanked by the beautiful hills, is a haven for wildlife, with many species present, the red kite in particular. Though nationally rare, the red kite seems to haunt this area and I have never spent a day in the valley around Rhandirmwyn without seeing at least one, and often many more.

The area was also the haunt of Twm Shon Catti, the Welsh Robin Hood, and his hideout cave is a little further up the valley. Ancient man has left his mark on the hills with cairns and standing stones placed to be seen from great distances. The old drovers also left their mark with the old drove-roads following the valley.

Rhandirmwyn may now be peaceful, but has in its past been a centre of industry. Perhaps it is now at its best since the pre-industrial age, and is definitely a wonderful place to unwind from the cares of modern life.

The Route

From the T-junction by the Royal Oak Inn and post office, head down a charming stream-sided lane past the Towy Pottery, the Nantymywyn Retreat of the Visitation of the Blessed Virgin Mary to Elizabeth (fancy having to write out that address on every letter you write!) and the solid and attractive church of St Barnabas (note the high number of infants' graves in the churchyard) down to the bridge over the River Towy.

1. Do not cross the bridge, but turn right into the field and follow the river bank northwards to the first gateway ahead. Do not go through the gate, but turn right and follow the field boundary, keeping the boundary on your left, to a pedestrian gate in the corner of the field. From the gate a path leads up by the trees, then left to join a track by the seemingly disused chapel. Turn right up the track to gain the lane.

2. Turn left up the lane and follow it for some 100 metres, where you climb a stile into the field on your right just past the trees. Bear diagonally left up the field, initially alongside the trees on a faint path, then through a belt of oaks across a field, to a gateway above a stand of oaks. Go through the gate on to a track which contours around the hill to the right.

   Ignore the branch of the track which goes right, but continue on the same line, the branch ahead fading out as you cross the bottom of a field above more oaks to a stile into the forestry ahead. Carry straight on along a moss-fringed forestry track down to a T-junction of forestry tracks above mine spoil at the now very visible Nant y Mai mine.

3. Turn right and follow the forestry track for some 300 metres to where the track starts to bear left, a little beyond where a new forestry track (not marked on the map) comes in from the right, and you will see a waymark with a yellow arrow which directs you up the bank to a narrow path up through the trees ahead. This path is followed for approximately 600 metres of climbing across a new, unmapped forestry track and up to a T-junction with a forestry track.

   Turn right to gain a major crossroads of forestry tracks and take

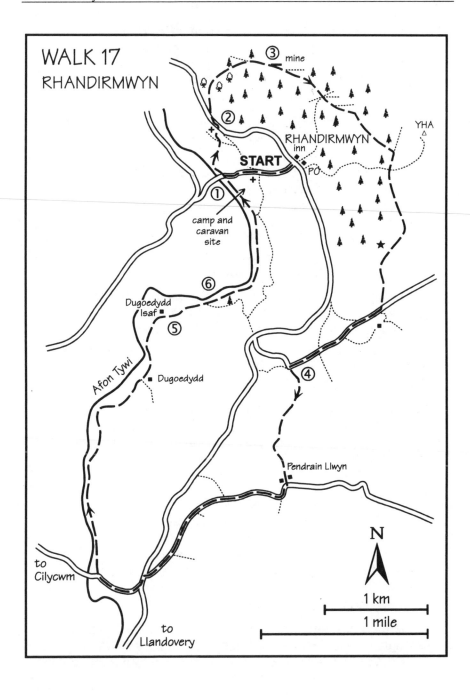

WALK 17
RHANDIRMWYN

③ mine

②

RHANDIRMWYN
inn

START

PO

YHA

①

camp and
caravan
site

⑥

Dugoedydd
Isaf

⑤

Afon Tywi

Dugoedydd

④

Pendrain Llwyn

to
Cilycwm

to
Llandovery

N

1 km

1 mile

the track opposite which leads you under Erw'r Hwch, where lead mining remains can be clearly seen. Continue for approximately three-quarters of a mile. The cairn of rocks on your right near the start of this section marks the start of a short cut back to Rhandirmwyn, while the main route gives good views over the valley.

About three-quarters of a mile from the crossroads of forestry tracks, the track takes a sharp left turn by the fence marking the edge of the forestry. Here you find a waymark to the nearby youth hostel. Follow this right down the track, alongside the fence and past the waymarked turn-off to the hostel where a right turn is way-marked down to Rhandirmwyn. Keep to the path between the open fields and the forestry. This takes you through a gate into a field where you first follow the edge of the forestry, then a line of marker posts to gain a grassy track round the left of a summit marked with an ancient cairn and stone.

Follow the track alongside the fence down to a sheepfold, where you go through a gate and then down the right-hand field boundary to a lane. This section offers superb views. Turn right on the lane and follow it for slightly more than half a mile to where the lane turns 90 degrees right. Abandon the lane here, going left through a gate on to a rough track heading south-west.

4. Follow this for some 200 metres until, just before the track opens up into fields, you take a right turn through a gate to follow a grassy track. Initially this is between a fence on the left and some trees on the right, then just alongside the left-hand fence, then becoming a hedged green lane.

At the end of the green lane section, by a waymark, turn left to cross a field with a fence on your right. Continue to a gate into another green lane section and then up to, and through, Pendrainll-wyn, a most attractive property, to a lane. Turn right on the lane, then right at a fork to start a prolonged section of surfaced road walking, following the lane downhill for almost a mile to the Llandovery to Rhandirmwyn road.

At the road turn left, then at the T-junction some 100 metres on, turn right on a lane signed to Cilycwm. Continue along this lane to a T-junction some 450 metres on, where you turn right up a lane marked as a dead end. This lane is followed parallel to the Afon Tywi for approximately one and a quarter miles, past a couple of properties and up to Dugoedydd Farm. Turn left along the rough track in front of the farm and follow this for some 600 metres, crossing open parkland to Dugoedydd Isaf, a substantial house.

5. The path goes over the stile to the right of the drive to the house and follows the left hedge of a field to reach the back of the house. Do not go through the gate into the large field, but keep the fence on your left and head in an easterly direction to a stile in the corner of a 'moon grass'-covered field.

    From the stile head in a more north-easterly direction to gain a stile into the woods, where a steep, narrow and faint path climbs diagonally across the wooded slope up to a stile onto a broad grass track. Follow the track for approximately 50 metres to a stile on your left which leads to steps down into the gorge where the Afon Tywi is a set of foaming rapids.

6. Turn right and follow a track for some 100 metres, then drop left on steps to a stile to the riverbank path. The riverbank is now followed for approximately one mile on a path that is well-waymarked and supplied with stiles. Sometimes you are inside, sometimes outside the riverbank fence, but eventually the path leads through the campsite to the bridge on the lane you descended at the start of the walk. Turn right to climb back up to the inn and shop.

18: Talley and Myndd Cynros

Distance: 4½ miles (7.25 km)

Time: 3 hours

Maps: OS Landranger 146 Lampeter Llandovery and Surrounding Area, OS Pathfinder 1036 Llandovery.

Start: Talley Abbey 632 327

Terrain: Mainly good field paths – can be muddy in places – one steep climb.

Nearest Town: Llandeilo

Parking: Limited parking at start of walk. Toilets nearby.

Public Transport: 2 buses per week from Llandeilo!

Refreshments: Pub, tea rooms, post office in Talley.

Stiles: 20

Suitable for: All. Dogs on leads. Some stiles may be difficult for dogs.

Along the way

This walk, though mainly notable for its stupendous views that stretch from the Brecon Beacons and Carmarthen Fans to way across Mid Wales, also takes in many points of historical and wildlife interest. An introduction to the history of Talley Abbey and the wildlife of the area can be found in Walk 7.

This walk passes much of interest to the nature lover, being home to many wild flowers, mammals and birds. During one walk along this four and a half mile route I saw buzzards, a red kite and a large dog fox that came to within six metres of me before running off, as well as traces of other wild animals.

Man has – as ever – left his mark. Notable remains passed on the route, apart from the abbey, include the abandoned silver/lead mine which stopped working around 1874/5 and the ruined farm of Blaen

Cwm Yr Efail, once home to a certain Talley schoolboy later to become Sir William Davies, in his day a noted editor of the Western Mail.

The steep pull up to the top of Mynydd Cynros offers many opportunities to stop and admire the view north, while the descent south is gentler and gives views over the Brecon Beacons National Park. Part of the route is on an old drove-road, while other parts are on quiet lanes fringed with trees and wild flowers in

Talley Abbey

wonderful surroundings. This peaceful corner of Carmarthenshire is so tranquil that you can understand the monks settling here for the quiet contemplation of God's wonders.

The Route

After exploring the abbey ruins, return to the road and turn right, following it northward past the newer church and on for some 1100 metres as this quiet lane climbs above the lakes.

1. A little before the lane arrives at the farm of Cilyllynfawr, the route leaves tarmac to start the climb up Mynydd Cynros, where a waymark points through a gate into a field on the left. Although there is not much path to be seen, keep the stream and field boundary on

your right as you climb, staying above the mature oak trees when the stream is lost in the depth of a ravine. Passing the remains of the silver/lead mine on your left, you will come to stiles over many cross fences on your way up to the corner of a modern coniferous plantation by the top of the hill.

2. Stopping to enjoy the views, you can gain breath and give thanks that the majority of climbing is done before you continue, keeping to the top of the woods until they drop away down to the left.

3. Continue along the field boundary around the front of the ruins of Blaen Cwm Yr Efail to a stile in the corner of the field. Cross the stile and cross the field ahead diagonally right to an inconspicuous stile in the middle of the opposite hedge. Cross this stile to drop diagonally left across the field to a stile just above the bottom corner.

4. After crossing this stile follow the fence right to a stile in the corner. Cross this into a green lane with fences both sides. Go along this green lane until it opens into a large field, then follow the right-hand boundary up to a gate in the far corner. Do not go through the gate but turn left and follow the hedge down to a gate and stile. Cross and follow the hedge, with the Brecon Beacons and Carmarthen Fans ahead.

   Continue along this hedge until you come to a waymark post, then bear left to the bottom hedge. Keep this on your right hand side until you come to a stile and gate in the far corner. Cross this and go straight ahead, bearing to the left of a boggy section and following the left-hand boundary to a gate and stile on to a track.

5. Turn right and go down the track right past a farm, bearing left at a track junction down to a narrow surfaced lane. Cross the lane and go through a metal gate opposite into a field, following the left-hand hedge over another gate and stile, then steeply down the left-hand field boundary and over a stile to a track.

6. Turn left and go through the gate into the farmyard and left along the track in front of the farmhouse and into a green lane. Follow this down through a gate by a metal shed and keep to it as it swings

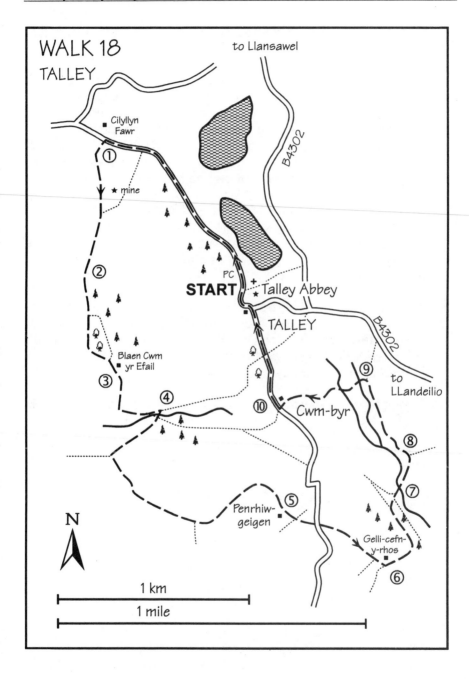

left above a coniferous plantation. Note how the track is cut out of solid rock.

7. This green track crosses a modern, bulldozed forestry track. Go through a gate and stile and on for some 50 metres to a waymark post. Drop steeply down right from the post to a stile and go right to a footbridge over the Afon Ig. Cross the footbridge and turn left, following the stream bank to a gate and stile on to a rough lane. Follow the lane up to a T-junction where you turn left, then right before the gate ahead, and down to the stream again.

8. Turn right over a stile by the stream and follow the bank, crossing two footbridges and stiles before coming to a third footbridge which, instead of crossing side streams, takes you back over the Afon Ig. Cross this bridge and a stile ahead into a somewhat damp field.

9. Follow the left-hand field boundary round to a track (the going may be boggy and you cross a drainage ditch) where you turn left, crossing the culverted Afon Ddu. Follow the track up to a waymark post. Here bear left across the stream, then follow the right-hand boundary and stream up to a gate on to a lane.

10. Turn right and follow the quiet lane back towards Talley. At the T-junction by Talley House turn left to regain the start of the walk.

19: Carreg Cennen and Carreglwyd

Distance: 9 miles (14.5 km)

Time: 4½ to 5 hours

Maps: OS Landrangers 159 Swansea and the Gower and 160 Brecon Beacons. OS Outdoor Leisure 12 Brecon Beacons West and OS Path-finders 1060 Llandeilo and Llangadog, and 1083 Ammanford and Brynamman.

Start: Carreg Cennen Castle car park 666 193 (public toilets).

Terrain: Mainly good paths and tracks with some road walking on generally quiet lanes.

Nearest Town: Llandeilo

Parking: See Start

Refreshments: Castell Farm at start

Stiles: 21

Suitable for: All good walkers. Dogs on leads in farmland, please.

Note: Some of the waymarked route diverges from the rights of way shown on OS Maps.

Along the way

Perched high above the Afon Cennen on a sheer 300ft limestone crag, Carreg Cennen Castle dominates the area and is visible from a great distance. It is probable that the site was in use long before the present castle structure was built as human remains, possibly prehistoric, have been discovered in the famous cave beneath the castle, and Roman coins found on the site.

The mediaeval castle is likely to have obliterated the remains of an Iron Age hill fort on the site, and despite its dramatic position and military strength, Carreg Cennen Castle saw little in the way of battle. It possibly appeared too strong to attack, or it was too far from the centre of national affairs to figure much. Despite this, it was a statement of power and the administrative and legal centre of the area.

The castle as we know it was not started until around 1289, although the site had long been fortified and fought over, first by the Welsh, then by the invading Normans. In 1416 Owain Glyndwr captured and damaged the castle, and after the Wars of the Roses the castle was deliberately wrecked to deny its shelter to robbers and rebels. This effectively ended the military life of Carreg Cennen Castle. However, even from around 1780, tourists started visiting the castle, with guided tours being recorded in 1804. One famous visitor was J.M.W. Turner who produced a very atmospheric painting of the castle in 1798.

Carreg Cennen from Castle View

The second Earl Cawdor (1817-1898) undertook some consolidation work and rebuilding, and in 1932 the castle was put in the care of HM Office of Works and is now maintained by Cadw on behalf of the State. A visit to the ruins is a must, one of the highlights being an exploration of the cave, which is natural and accessed by a clifftop gallery. It is full of limestone formations and served the castle as a water source and dovecote!

Tickets to the castle are purchased at Castle Farm at Carreg Cennen. Here there is a tea shop, souvenir shop and a rare breeds trust, and as you sit outside taking tea, various fowl – ducks, geese, chickens and a peacock – wander around. Cattle such as Longhorn, Welsh Black and White Peak (said to be the descendants of the fairy cattle of Llyn y Fan Fach legend) as well as Balwen sheep and other breeds are to be seen on the farm. Much in demand as 'period' extras in historical film work, the animals have been seen in major TV and film productions, the farmer and his family also appearing in roles as animal handlers. The tea room is recommended, not least for its friendly service, and torches can be hired here to help you explore the cave.

Carreg Cennen is not the only fortification seen on this walk. From the ridge above Carreglwyd you look down on the extensive remains of Y Gaer Fach and Y Gaer Fawr, crowning the summits of Garn Goch. Among the most impressive hill forts in Wales, they clearly show the lines of now-fallen drystone walls that were the hills' Iron Age defences between 700BC and AD43.

In this predominantly limestone area the wildlife is varied and interesting, with some rare plants such as spiked speedwell and whitebeam to be discovered. The woods surrounding the castle are both an SSSI and a Nature Reserve, and show a change in the tree cover from ash and hazel on the slopes below the castle to oak on the eastern edge of the ridge. This is due to a sudden change of the underlying rock from limestone to sandstone on the ridge. There is a good variety in both flora and fauna to be seen, with a good possibility of spotting red kites, while buzzards, curlews and larks abound.

The views from this walk over the Black Mountain, as well as Mid Wales, are extensive and stunning.

The Route

From the car park head up towards the castle, passing through the farmyard by the tea shop. Passing a pillory(!) and going through two gates, you come up to the ticket collector's kiosk by the castle entrance.

1. Here you have a choice of turning right to visit the castle, or going straight on through the gate to follow the walk. The walk takes you down a well-maintained path into oak woods and across a footbridge spanning the stream, before climbing up alongside a tributary on a good path that develops into a green lane.

2. This eventually leads you up to a set of wooden steps and a stile on to a farm track at a track junction. Go straight ahead on the main track as it zigzags up the bank ahead. At a junction some 200 metres up the track, double back on yourself on the left-hand option.

    Follow this track up past a barn and into a field where the track peters out, then bear left (east) to a gate and stile in the left fence. Crossing into the next field, follow the left-hand fence over some ruins and swing right to a gate and stile with a waymark by the right-hand end of the ruins.

3. Cross to a somewhat wet and boggy grass track that leads you up into a field. Cross the field to a stile and gate, following the line on which you came up. This leads you on to the lower slopes of the open hill. Follow the left-hand hedge to join a good track just beyond a cottage that must have superb views!

    Follow the track down to where it joins the unfenced mountain road, then turn left on the road and follow this to a T-junction just beyond a sheepfold and cattle grid.

4. Turn left, signposted to Llandeilo. Follow this quiet lane for approximately three quarters of a mile, dropping down a charming dingle alongside a stream full of water-sculpted rocks to Pont Parc Owen, a delightful spot. Climb steeply again, past Parc Owen Farm.

5. One hundred metres past the turn on your left signed 'Tynywaun',

WALK 19
CARREG CENNEN AND CARREGLWYD

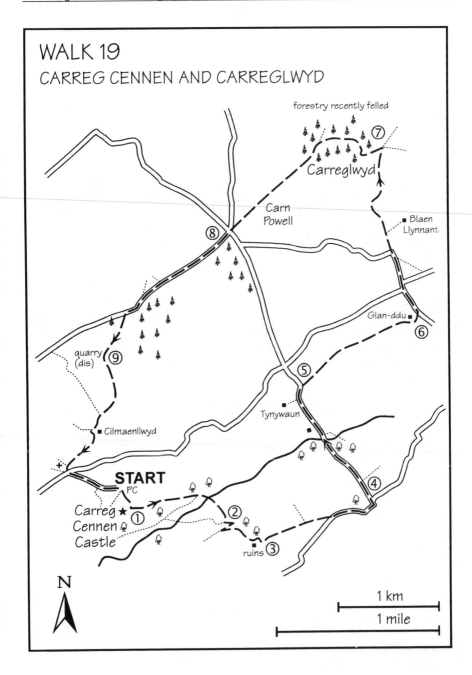

forestry recently felled

Carreglwyd

⑦

Carn
Powell

■ Blaen
Llynnant

⑧

Glan-ddu ■

⑥

quarry ⑨
(dis)

Tynywaun

⑤

■ Cilmaenllwyd

START
PC

④

Carreg ★ ①
Cennen
Castle

②

ruins ③

N

1 km

1 mile

turn right along a track signed to Glan-Ddu. Follow this to where it ends by a railway box-car shed. Go through the gate ahead and follow the right-hand hedge across a couple of fields and up to a double fence on top of a small bank.

Cross the stiles here and follow the left-hand hedge down past Glan-Ddu Farm to a gate and stile below the farmyard which lead you to a farm track.

6. Turn right on the track down to the lane, where you turn left. Follow the lane almost due south for some 750 metres, passing a chapel and two junctions to Trap and Gwynfe (follow signs for Fairfach). When you come to a farm drive going straight on when the lane swings left, take the farm drive. Where this swings right after 200 metres, go straight on up a track which climbs up to the ridge at Bwlch y Gors.

7. From the junction of tracks at the Bwlch, bear left on the main track and through a gate into what was until relatively recently a coniferous plantation. Follow the forestry track as it dips towards the ruins of the 17th-century buildings of Garreg-Llwyd. This section of the walk looks down on the clearly visible hill forts on Carn Goch.

At track junctions bear left, uphill, until you cross a boundary on to rough pasture under the rocky outcrops of Carn Powell. Follow the right-hand fence, on the flank of the ridge, and a faint track going south-west when the fence turns off right. Continue down to a lane junction by a coniferous plantation.

8. Take the minor lane running ahead along the north side of the plantation and follow this for almost a mile, to just beyond the forestry track on the west side of a second plantation. Here a plank bridge over the ditch and a stile lead you into a rather wet field of tussock grass. Cross this diagonally, almost due south, following the waymark fingerpost signed to Cilmaen-Llwyd and Castle View. You will come to a gate and stile in a stone wall. These lead you into an old quarry, which you cross on a faint path heading south-west between two unusually linear pits to meet a wall. Turn right and follow the wall to two gates and a stile.

9. Cross the stile and head south, following the right-hand fence, until, after traversing a cross fence, you drop down the middle of the field on about the same line to a gate and stile in the corner. Once over you are on a farm track which leads you down to Cilmaen-Llwyd farmyard.

Go past the end of the farmhouse to a gate and stile in the corner which lead on to a green lane that swings round behind the farmhouse and down to the road between Castle View Farm and the Llwyn y Ronen Wesleyan Chapel. Turn left, then immediately right, down the lane signed to Carreg Cennen Castle. This leads you back to the start of the walk and a well-earned cup of tea!

20: Mynydd Llanfihangel – Rhos-y-Corn and Gwernogle

Distance: 9 miles (14.5 km)

Time: 4 to 5 hours

Maps: OS Landranger 146 Lampeter, Llandovery and Surrounding Area and OS Pathfinder 1035 Pencader.

Start: Moorland road junction 501 354

Terrain: Mainly good forestry tracks, some road walking. In some places the path is muddy and/or indistinct. Strenuous.

Nearest Town: Llandysul

Parking: Limited roadside parking at start.

Public Transport: None

Refreshments: None

Stiles: None

Suitable for: Hardy walkers who can follow a map and directions in difficult and confusing terrain. Dogs on leads around livestock. Beware of forestry operations in progress.

Along the way

While the open slopes of Mynydd Llanfihangel – Rhos-y-Corn offer superb views across Wales, even as far as the Brecon Beacons and wild Mid Wales, most of this walk is through part of the Brechfa Forest.

Mostly planted by the Forestry Commission in the 1940s, there are still remnants of broad-leaved woods to be found, recalling the mediaeval hunting forest which, in its heyday, had its own court and laws. The forest was not only used for hunting, but also for charcoal production, an industry that survived up to the end of the First

World War, along with bark stripping for the leather tanning trade. Naphtha for the armaments trade was produced locally in wartime, while timber production for pulp etc. is the modern use for the forest.

Recreation is also an important function of these forests today, and the broad, well-surfaced tracks provide easy walking, while, although not as rich as in the 15th century when roebuck, harts, stags, falcons, bees, herons and red

Descending by Afon Marlais

squirrel abounded, there is a wide variety of fauna and flora to be found.

Parts of this walk follow old tramways used, I understand, during the planting of the modern forest, while many attractive old stone buildings are passed along the ancient lanes and tracks followed. The open-minded may like to consider the plausibility of the bridge at Pont Cwmmawr-Du being haunted by a lady in white, and reports of a UFO landing near our route at Gwernogle!

The Route

From the road junction near the OS trig column set into the remains of an ancient cairn, take the road almost due west towards the obvious fire watch tower, near which is another cairn, Cryg y Bedw. Before you get this far, you cross a cattle grid and turn left off the road down a forestry track which is more grassy than most.

1. Note the 'walkers welcome' plaque on the gate as you start down the track. It's nice to know you are wanted! The track is followed down the valley of the Afon Marlais, which can be heard and occasionally seen down to your left. For about three miles you can also see the open hillside on the far side of the valley, but from then on the trees cover both slopes. At this stage of the walk navigation is easy and you follow the riverside track for around two and a half miles on the west bank before coming to a track junction.

2. Turn left here, the first left turn off the track you have been following, and cross the Afon Marlais to the east bank. Follow the track as it climbs gently south-eastwards, away from the river and up to a road after about three-quarters of a mile.

3. By the road is an old and quite large shed, the open half of which offers shelter in poor weather. The ends of some tram rails are still visible under the doors. This shed, once used as a treatment plant for creosoting fence posts, is condemned and could soon disappear. However, this area is to be developed as a picnic site and should still offer a place to rest.

   On reaching the road, turn left, then immediately leave it again for a track. Do not go up the gated forestry track straight ahead, but take the less obvious fork left that goes parallel to the road for a short distance before swinging right by Keeper's Lodge.

   Follow this track past some cottages and through two gates, where it becomes a very pleasant, if occasionally muddy, path along the bottom of the woodland. Keep to this well-used bridleway and pass through two hunters' gates. The path becomes a green lane or track, fords a small stream and climbs up to a gate to a farm track. Turn right and descend to a quiet lane. Turn left and follow this lane for a little more than a quarter of a mile to the aforementioned haunted bridge.

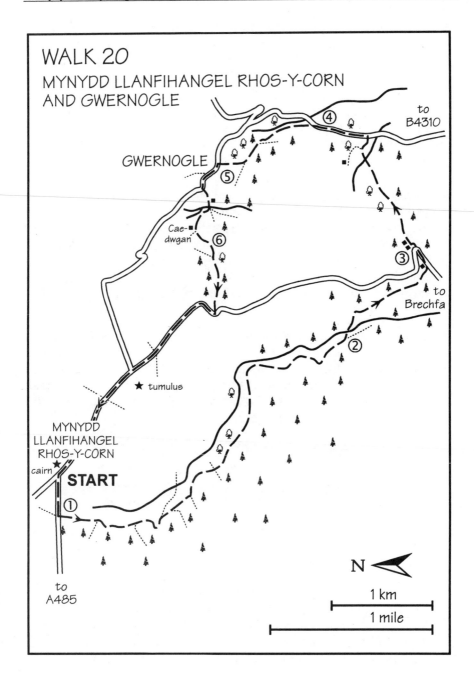

WALK 20
MYNYDD LLANFIHANGEL RHOS-Y-CORN
AND GWERNOGLE

to
B4310

GWERNOGLE

④

⑤

Cae-
dwgan

⑥

③

to
Brechfa

★ tumulus

②

MYNYDD
LLANFIHANGEL
RHOS-Y-CORN

cairn ★
START

①

N ◀

to
A485

1 km

1 mile

4. Leave the road at the bend by the bridge for a track that goes straight ahead and up through the trees, almost parallel to and above the river Clydach. Attractive bathing pools can be seen in the narrow gorge below. This is, it seems, one of the old tramways used in the afforestation of the area and is followed for some three-quarters of a mile, bearing right when you reach a T-junction of tracks. Your next objective is a very easily missed junction with no waymarks. This is some 100 metres past the obvious T-junction and is by a solitary oak tree on the right of the path.

Turn right here down to a gateway, from where an indistinct and rather boggy path leads diagonally left down through more open woodland to the edge of a rough pasture. There is a cottage below with a large 'wall' of solar panels. (This is where the UFO is said to have landed in the 1970s.) Drop down across the field and to the right of the cottage to gain a track. Follow this right, past a shed, to footbridges across two streams and up to the road at Gwernogle.

5. Turn left on to this road and go through the village (noting the plaque to Tomos Glyn Cothi 1764-1833, the famous preacher and hymn writer) and out the other side. Approximately 100 metres past the bridge in the village there is a road junction. Take the left turn – signed as a dead end – and follow this for approximately 300 metres to a ford with two footbridges.

Cross the first footbridge then turn right up a track. This immediately forks and the left fork is followed up an ancient track cut into the bedrock. The track swings around the north side of a small valley, passes an old farm and drops to a spring before climbing up into the conifer woods.

6. Between the farm and the woods you may find the route indistinct, muddy and blocked with fences. Follow the lower boundary of the field beyond the spring, then climb diagonally across the field to the far top corner, where a track enters the trees. Once you gain the woods the path is clear and climbs up to a deserted farmyard. Turn left here to gain the road. Turn right on the road which climbs up on to the open hill and leads you back to the start of the walk.

21: Bethlehem and Carn Goch

Distance: 6 miles (9.6 km)

Time: 3 to 4 hours

Maps: OS Landrangers 160 Brecon Beacons, 146 Lampeter, Llandovery and Surrounding Area and 157 Swansea and the Gower. OS Pathfinder 1060 Llandeilo and Llangadog and OS Outdoor Leisure 12 Brecon Beacons, Western Area.

Start: Bethlehem post office 684 252

Terrain: Mainly good tracks and field paths. Muddy in places. One steep ascent. Some road walking on quiet lanes.

Nearest Town: Llandeilo

Parking: Limited roadside parking in Bethlehem. Small car park at the post office.

Refreshments: Bethlehem post office

Stiles: 6

Suitable for: Nearly everyone, though stamina is needed for the climb up to Carn Goch.

My thanks to Mr G Richards at the post office in Bethlehem for his help with information on the famous post office, and to Mrs Jones at Carregfoelgam Farm who advised me to direct walkers down the green lanes around her property to avoid using the path through the farmyard with its possible inconvenience to both the work of the farm and to walkers. Thanks also to staff of the Brecon Beacons National Park for their help in researching and planning this walk.

Along the way

Bethlehem has a special place in the story of Welsh Christmases. Although only one of a few Bethlehems in Wales, all of course named

The view from the side of Carn Goch

after Christ's birthplace, the Bethlehem near Llangadog and Llandeilo offers a unique hand-franked and hand-dated postmark 'Llythyrdy Bethlehem'. This very collectable postmark is welcomed by thousands around the globe and the little post office is a year-round tourist attraction, with Christmas post being taken to Bethlehem at any time of the year and postmarked ready for a special mobile post office to turn up. First-day covers of the new Christmas stamps are attached to the mail and the seasonally decorated envelopes are posted to all corners of the world in time for Christmas Day.

Special Christmas cards and postcards are available in the post office, featuring pictures of the famous building. The postcard also shows Robert the postie collecting the mail. With his picture travelling worldwide, Robert must be the most famous postman in the world, but has not let this, nor the lack of any monetary recognition, change his lifestyle.

The franking of letters with the Bethlehem mark almost came to an end in the post office's 'rationalisation' following privatisation in the 1980s. Soon after Mr and Mrs Richards took it over in 1988, the 'powers that be' closed the post office in Bethlehem and removed all the equipment, leaving only the collecting box. Post left in the box was merely collected for sorting and franking in Swansea. However, when the popularity of Bethlehem was brought to their attention, the Post Office agreed to set up a special mobile post office for just eight hours in the run-up to Christmas to deal with first-day covers.

Following representations by the public and to maintain the unique mailing service which had been operated by Royal Mail at Bethlehem, Llandeilo since 1 December 1966, Mr Richards took legal advice and hired a patent agent to come up with the now famous 'Llythyrdy – Bethlehem' rubber stamp. The Post Office agree that Mr and Mrs Richards have every right to stamp letters, cards and first-day covers.

Visitors from all over the world – Algeria, Finland, Faeroes, British Columbia, Patagonia, Trinidad (and even the original Bethlehem) – come to deposit their Christmas mail at all times of the year, and from May onwards there is a huge pile of mail bearing the famous mark awaiting the arrival of the special post office and the first-day cover Christmas stamps.

Recipients of the famous postmark include Mrs Clinton, wife of the President of the USA, who caused many man hours to be spent by investigators searching for the meaning of Llythyrdy (P.O.) – although Mrs Clinton has Welsh connections it was first thought to be a Hebrew word. The USA has now been educated and has learned at least one Welsh word! Other recipients include HM The Queen, John Major and Gary Glitter, while the President of China was sent a Bethlehem-stamped letter written in Latin.

For those interested in statistics, it appears that more mail bearing the stamp is forwarded to Holland than any other continental country, while the highest percentage goes to the USA. Most visitors to the post office come from the South Wales valleys, are male and are members of the teaching or nursing professions.

A visit, with your Christmas cards ready, is recommended at any time of year. The post office and tea shop being open nearly every day, Monday to Saturday, and some Sundays (closed Thursdays) from 9.00 to 17.00, and even later in the height of the season. Mr Richards is a mine of information, will happily chat for hours and show you the visitors' book full of the names of visitors from the world over. When full, the book is to be donated to the National Library of Wales. For those unable to visit in person, arrangements can be made by post (!) to Llythyrdy (P.O.), Bethlehem, Llandeilo, SA19 9YH, or by telephoning 01550 777331.

A cheering Christmas tale of success and of spreading a bit of happiness in a rather gloomy world. Of course, the post office and its rubber stamp are comparatively recent arrivals here and man lived in this area thousands of years before a postal service was even thought of, and even before the original Bethlehem saw its most famous son born.

The Iron Age forts of Carn Goch which dominate this walk date back to around 500BC to AD43 and appear to have had several functions, ranging from defence for the elite of society to being secure cattle enclosures. The two forts on Carn Goch, Y Gaer Fach and Y Gaer Fawr, make up the largest Iron Age hill fort in Wales.

Y Gaer Fawr most probably had an important political role in the region, with defences that were – and still are – very impressive, symbolising power and prestige as well as military might and strategic importance. Enclosing an area of approximately 23 acres and with an unfinished extension of nine acres, the fort holds the foundations of circular huts, while outside enclosures point to cereal cultivation.

There appear to have been three phases of construction to this steep-sided plateau hill fort with the first stage being visible in the earthen bank at the eastern end. Phase two included the massive stone built defences, and phase three the nine-acre extension. There were about eight entrances to the fort: the main one to the east with stone towers, a wooden bridge and a wooden gate, while some of the six posterns are still visible and stone-lined.

As well as Y Gaer Fach, thought to be associated with Y Gaer Fawr, there is a third fort to the west-north-west of Carn Goch and several nearby cairns and standing stones, while under the south-east ramparts of Y Gaer Fach there is a stone cairn circle. This area also saw Roman occupation and the route passes near the site of a Roman villa, though no trace of this can be made out from the walk.

There is a great variety of plant life, with the spring and summer hedges a riot of colour. Bird life is equally varied and you may well see buzzards and kites as well as more common species. The last time I covered this route I was privileged to see a barn owl silently swoop over the fields – in the middle of a warm and bright sunny day!

The forts dominate this walk, but compete for attention with superb views over the Towy Valley and north to Mid Wales.

The Route

From the Bethlehem post office, head back uphill for about 50 metres to a farm driveway. A waymarked footpath runs up the drive to the farmyard, round the back of the farmhouse and through a gate into a field. Turn right and follow the right-hand boundary to a gate and stile on to the lane by a chapel. Here there is good parking, making this an alternative start if there is no room to park in Bethlehem itself.

1. Turn right and follow the lane downhill to a bridge over the stream by a very attractive holiday home.

2. Just by the bridge, a waymark points you left over a stile into a field which you go straight across to a gap in the boundary opposite, by some obvious trees. This is a permissive path, avoiding the actual right of way that runs through the farm.

   From the gap, follow the right-hand boundary of a tumbled wall and rowan trees up to a stile into the woods ahead and the start of a long, stiff climb – slippery when wet – up to Carn Goch. At first the path is indistinct, but it climbs up inside the right-hand side of the woods. Crossing a ruinous cross wall, it bears a little right to climb out of the woods on to a more visible, meandering path up bracken and bilberry-covered slopes to the saddle between Y Gaer Fach and Y Gaer Fawr.

3. Coming to a broad, grassy path running left to right, turn right to explore the smaller fort, or left to follow the main route over Y Gaer Fawr. Follow the obvious path through the fort's defences and on to the 23-acre defended plateau, exploring this impressive Iron Age site before continuing along the path over the eastern end and down to a farm track at a track junction.

4. Turn right and follow the track up through a gate. Some 50 metres beyond the gate, cross a stile on your left into a narrow green lane which climbs to rejoin the track beyond the farm to your right. Follow the track up past a ruined stables until, after approximately 500 metres, you reach a rectangular enclosure where several tracks join.

5. Leave this enclosure by the green lane running north-east from the top left corner, staying on this route for approximately one and a quarter miles as it drops gradually down across the hillside, ignoring waymarked footpaths that run off it.

   In places the track is very clear, in others a little overgrown or muddy, but eventually, after crossing above a Forestry Commission plantation, it drops down to a wooded stream and turns abruptly left.

6. Follow the track down and where it becomes a surfaced farm lane, continue north to a crossroads of quiet lanes. If you look left as you approach the junction, you look over the site of the Roman villa, just north of some cottages.

7. At the junction, turn left and follow the lane for about one and a quarter miles back to Bethlehem, ignoring side turns, until you come to a major T-junction by the school in Bethlehem. Turn left to drop back down to the post office and the start of the walk.

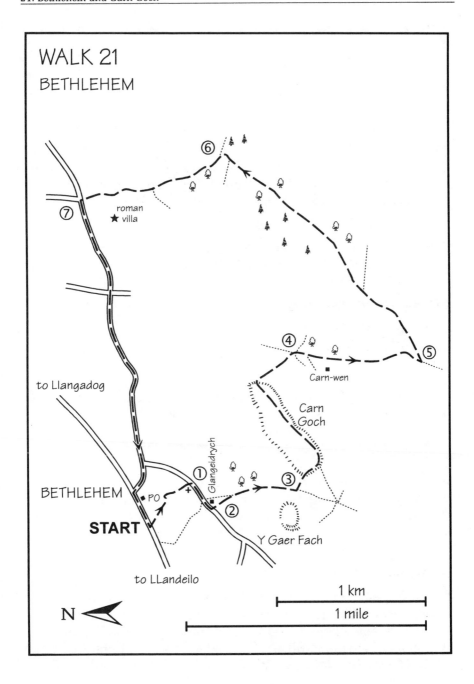

WALK 21
BETHLEHEM

22: Mynydd Myddfai and Arosfa

Distance: 10 miles (16 km)

Time: 5 to 6 hours

Maps: OS Landranger 160 Brecon Beacons, OS Pathfinders 1060 Llandeilo and Llangadog and 1061 Senny Bridge and Outdoor Leisure 12 Brecon Beacons National Park Western Area.

Start: Car park Pont'Ar Wysg 819 271

Terrain: High open moorland (often pathless) and forestry tracks. Wet and boggy in places. Some shallow fords may be more than walking-boot deep in wet weather.

Nearest Town: Llandovery

Parking: See Start

Refreshments: None

Stiles: 4

Suitable for: Walkers who are confident in their navigational and route finding abilities. This is a serious high-level walk and all proper hill walking clothing and equipment should be taken.

Note: Not all of this walk is on rights of way, but is on land generally accepted as 'open' for walking without having to gain permission from the landowners first. I am indebted to National Park staff for their help in researching and planning this walk.

Along the way

Crossing a wild and ancient landscape, this walk gives some of the finest views in Carmarthenshire and, to enjoy it to its fullest, should be walked only when visibility is at its best. Encompassing the Carmarthen Fans to the south, the Brecon Beacons to the south-east, the Black Mountains to the south-west and Mid Wales and the Cam-

Cairn, north of Fedw Fawr

brian Mountains, as well as the Towy Valley, there are excellent views to be had from almost every point on the walk. To take this route in poor weather is to miss out on one of its most attractive features, reducing it to a rather dull navigational exercise.

The start of the walk leads you up beside the infant River Usk and over the rolling moorland below Fan Brycheiniog where the river marks the far eastern border of Carmarthenshire. At the end of the Ice Age, water levels would have been higher, cutting a deep V-shaped valley. Later, when water levels dropped, the reduced river flattened the valley bottom. In wet weather the river can easily flood over the lower, flat areas.

This wild borderland is dotted with prehistoric remains, two stone circles and a cairn being just discernible over the border in Glamorganshire up the Nant Tarw. Further along the walk, on Mynydd Myddfai, several ancient cairns are passed, including 'Tomen y Rhos'. These are typical of upland Bronze Age burial cairns and date back to 1800-1200BC.

The Romans also have left their mark in the area and the walk crosses the Roman marching camp at Arosfa, built some time in the first century AD. Designed to give rudimentary defences and shaped like a playing card, a marching camp was intended to give protection every night to soldiers using the nearby road. This kind of camp was often built in a matter of hours and constructed by the soldiers themselves, between finishing a day's march and settling down for the night. Although little can now be seen of the outer fortifications built so long ago, a careful eye will be able to pick out the low banks of this camp as you cross them.

A number of the hillside tracks on this walk would appear to be fairly ancient, from possibly Roman or prehistoric times, with some showing signs of more recent use such as the old carriage road met at Pen y Bylchau near an ancient enclosure.

The intermittently visible linear earthwork that runs for approximately three miles along the south-east flank of Mynydd Myddfai is probably the remains of an 18th/19th-century tile stone quarry. The tiles would have been used for roofing houses and farm buildings before the ubiquitous slates were imported for this purpose from North Wales.

The Glasfynydd Forest is in many ways a fairly typical Forestry Commission conifer plantation, but has several areas where native broadleaf trees survive, notable in little dingles crossed by this walk. This provides variety, while its setting around the Usk Reservoir adds significant interest. The reservoir itself was opened by the Queen in July 1955 to provide water for Swansea, but now has an added role as a recreational facility. Numerous anglers will be seen on its banks, while birdwatchers have hides dotted around from which to view the aquatic birds, such as the tufted duck, which are protected in the reservoir's Conservation Area,

Llyn y Fan Fach, in the shadow of the cliffs of the Carmarthen Fans, seen to the south, is home to a curious legend, famous in the area. Although I have heard various versions, the basic theme is as follows. A farmer's son from nearby Myddai, to the north-west of this walk, was in the habit of grazing his mother's cows on the slopes around Llyn y Fan Fach, and one day happened to see a beautiful maiden sitting on the surface of the lake. Naturally, he fell in love with her.

By way of introduction he offered her his lunch and asked her to marry him. Saying she was no easy catch, she spurned his love and lunch remarking that the bread was too hard. Not easily put off, the lad returned the next day with some raw dough (a bit of an over-reaction to my mind) and offered both it and marriage to the lass. Again he was rejected (as was the bread) and the maid disappeared back into the pool.

Being determined, the lad tried a third time, the next day taking up some freshly baked bread (good thinking this!) which was accepted along with his offer of wedded bliss (third time lucky!). The maiden left the pool and, taking with her a herd of fairy cattle, went with our hero to be his wife. However, she warned her betrothed that if he ever struck her three times with iron, she would return to the lake and leave him for good.

Many years of wedded happiness passed and this fairy maid presented her husband with three lusty sons, and with fairy cattle on the pastures, the farm did well and prospered. Unfortunately, over the years, by bad luck, bad temper and bad memory, the foolish fellow managed to hit his wife with iron a total of three times, and off she went to the first recorded refuge for battered wives – the lake – taking with her the herd of prize fairy cattle.

Naturally, her husband and sons were heartbroken and the boys took to hanging around their mother's watery home. Naturally, without the fairy cattle and with three-quarters of the farm's manpower languishing about the lake, the farm started to fail. Taking pity on her boys, their fairy mother gave them a leather pouch containing the secrets of healing and taught them herbalism to provide them with a future as doctors or healers.

The boys and their descendants became famous as healers, the last known direct descendant being, in fact, a Dr C Rice-Williams who practised medicine in Aberystwyth in 1891. The damp damsel was never seen again. Although just the bones of the legend, you can see in the above story hints of prehistoric Bronze Age/Iron Age tribal conflicts and integration, Celtic water spirit worship, as well as a tale of romance which is ethnologically intriguing.

During the course of this walk you will cross several differing environments, and the plant life and wildlife naturally varies widely. You are likely to see herons, buzzards, ravens – even possibly the red kite – over the open hillside, while a wide variety of birds are to be seen on the reservoir. Gorse, bilberry and bedstraws mingle with the moorland grasses, while orchids, foxgloves and a mass of other flowers can be found around the sides of the reservoir.

A mixture of ancient and more modern features of wild landscape and man-made forest, this walk is mostly a fine moorland walk notable for its superb views, and dominated by the Carmarthen Fan summits which are almost always visible.

The Route

From the car park area, cross the road and follow a faint track made by wheeled vehicles up the western side of the River Usk, keeping above the low-lying, rather boggy areas. Follow the riverside for approximately one and a quarter miles, splashing across the fords of Dunant Wysg and Nant y Lloi until, when the path has practically disappeared, you come to where the river valley turns in a more south-easterly direction and the smaller stream, the Nant Cwmothlwyn, joins it from the south-west.

1. Turn away from the river here, or a little way up the Nant Cwmothlwyn, and head north-west, picking up the faintest of tracks over the flank of a small hillock. This leads you down to a boggy ford. From the ford the track keeps heading north-west, becoming more defined as it drops down to ford the Afon Llechach.

2. After fording the Llechach for a second time, crossing back onto its east side just above the rocks of Tomen Llechach, abandon the track and head straight up the hillside ahead, in a roughly north-north-easterly direction. This takes you across the Roman marching camp (bear to the right of the central boggy area) and you will need to keep your eyes peeled to make out the low banks. Keep to this line and you will come down to the minor road, possibly of ancient origin, by Bylchau Blaenclydach.

   Cross the road and drop down in a roughly north-north-west direction across the charming hollow of Bryn yr Wyn and up to the summit of Fedw Fawr on trackless moorland.

3. Continue on the same (pathless) heading as you drop steeply down the far slope of Fedw Fawr and head uphill by way of an ancient, despoiled cairn to a small saddle on the ridge of Mynydd Myddfai. Ignore the many confusing sheep paths that entice you off your line.

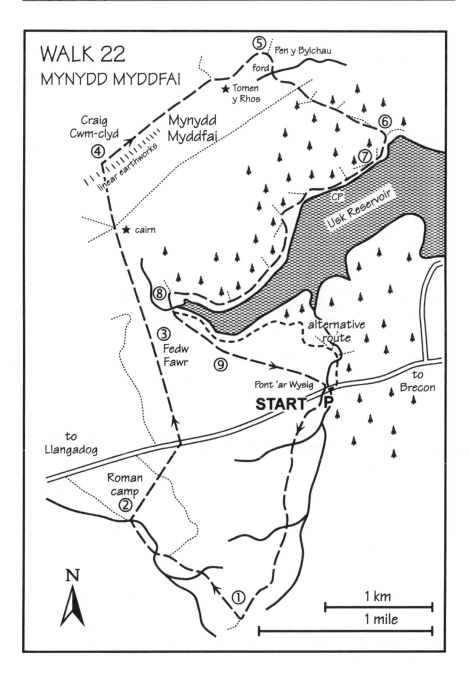

WALK 22
MYNYDD MYDDFAI

Pen y Bylchau
ford
★ Tomen y Rhos

Craig
Cwm-clyd
④
Mynydd
Myddfai
linear earthworks

⑥
⑦
CP
Usk Reservoir

★ cairn

⑧
alternative route

③
Fedw
Fawr
⑨

to Brecon

Pont 'ar Wysig
START P

to
Llangadog

Roman
camp
②

①

N

1 km
1 mile

4. Crossing part of the linear earthwork in a rather boggy area, you gain the ridge of the hill to be greeted by superb views. Turn right along the ridge and follow it north-east for about three-quarters of a mile, passing a trig point and the cairn of Tomen Y Rhos to join the old carriage road, a well-defined track.

5. Follow the track right and at the track junction, turn right, dropping southwards, crossing a ford and staying on the track as it enters the forest.

6. Once in the forest keep to the main track, ignoring all side turnings, as it goes roughly east-south-east, heading for Pen y Fan in the distance. Eventually, after some 800 metres, you come out on a surfaced road by the reservoir. Turn right.

7. By the car park at the end of this road, head up right on a forestry track. At the second gate, a little way on, take the track which branches off left and contours around the north side of the reservoir.

8. Follow this winding track for about a mile until, at the far western end of the reservoir, the track swings south, crosses a footbridge and then swings east again. To follow the main route, just as the track swings west, leave it for the open hill by way of a stile over the fence.

Alternatively, stay on the forestry track as it winds through the trees and, if you bear right at all junctions, this will lead you back to the road by Pont'ar Wysg. Turn right on the road and cross the bridge to regain the car park. This alternative route strays a few metres outside Carmarthenshire, crossing the county border when it crosses the River Usk.

9. On the main route, follow the edge of the forestry over the flank of Fedw Fawr to a corner where the forest fence swings north-east. From this corner, head roughly east-south-east across Bryn Pwllygerwn, over trackless moorland for a little over half a mile to reach the starting point.

23: Mynydd Ddu

Distance: 5 miles (8 km)

Time: 2 to 3 hours

Maps: OS Landranger 160 Brecon Beacons, OS Pathfinders 1083 Ammanford and Brynamman and 1060 Llandeilo and Llangadog and OS Outdoor Leisure 12 Brecon Beacons National Park Western Area.

Start: Car park 732 187. Although marked on the map as having toilets, these no longer exist.

Terrain: Mainly rough quarry tracks and an ancient 'Roman' road. Steep, loose rock in places, boggy in others. Some strenuous ascents.

Nearest Town: Brynamman

Parking: At Start

Refreshments: None

Stiles: None

Suitable for: Walkers who are confident in their navigational abilities, route finding and ability to descend broken rock slopes. This is a serious high-level walk and all proper hillwalking clothing and equipment should be taken.

Note: Not all this route is on rights of way, but is on land generally accepted as 'open' for walking without having to gain permission from the landowner first. I am indebted to the National Park staff for their help in researching and planning this walk.

Along the way

Such is the nature of this walk that it has to be considered wasteful, if not merely more navigationally difficult, and even hazardous, to take the route in any but the finest weather with clear visibility. The views take in most of the wildest parts of the Brecon Beacons, as well as extending north over Mid Wales and the Cambrian Mountains, and south over Swansea Bay to Exmoor and the Devon coast, with plenty to catch the eye, such as Carreg Cennen Castle.

The walk passes by and even follows sites of historic and prehistoric interest, with industrial archaeology dominating to a degree. Much quarrying has taken place in this part of the National Park, though now the quarries are abandoned and their harsh lines are being rendered softer and more attractive as the land heals its scars. Few people can fail to appreciate the grandeur of the sheer limestone edges of the rugged north-facing quarries on Foel Fawr, or fail to enjoy the now softened contours of the Clogau Bach and Clogau Mawr faces.

The quarries on Foel Fawr were worked as late as the 1930s and provided considerable employment for the local area, though working on the faces in winter must have been hard indeed as they catch the full force of the weather, including the prevailing winter storm winds from the north!

These quarries, with their limestone faces, are visited by the occasional climber, and, as they also boast a cave entrance, by those who do their climbing in the dark, underground! Hang-gliders and parapenters sometimes take off for the skies from these slopes. School and university parties also visit the quarries on historical, archaeological, geographical and geologically-themed visits, so there is, it seems, something for everyone here.

There are the remains of old limekilns, where the rock was burned to produce the quicklime used for making mortar and as a fertiliser to sweeten the soil of farms on more acid soils. Some of the other quarries are more like sloping-sided sand pits and were used in the past for the extraction of silica sand. This was used as an industrial cleaner, being a highly abrasive form of broken down millstone grit which is, along with limestone, one of the predominant rocks in the area.

The limestone areas are notable for their pleasant turf and 'shake holes', depressions on the surface where the limestone below has been eroded by underground streams, while the millstone grit areas are boggier as they drain less well.

As well as the quarries and sand pits, man has left his mark in other ways. Most of the summits in the area boast substantial cairns.

Carn Pen Rhiw Ddu, Mynydd Ddu

These cairns are not always on the highest point, but are sited to dominate a huge area and be visible to a degree that belies their size.

Part of this walk follows a public bridleway which traces its route north from Brynamman, aiming for Llangadog. Known locally as the 'Roman road', this is an ancient trackway that greatly predates the Roman occupation, although the Romans almost certainly improved and used this route. This track was still in regular use in the 1930s, with the inhabitants of Capel Gwynfe to the north taking it to travel to Brynamman in the south. This would have been a full day's outing, an exciting trip which could include a visit to the new and even more exciting cinema. Now the track is used only for recreation, but is still remarkable for its ease of walking and its well-engineered surface and route.

Despite a lack of maintenance, the path is obvious, in places cutting into the side of the slope, in others being banked up to give an even width. Where the surface has been cleared of rocks, they are piled at the sides to form 'kerbs', and the track bends and veers to avoid bogs (as much as possible) and to take easy angles on the slopes. Although the track is now a bit boggy in places where it cuts across the natural drainage streams, it is a marvel of ancient engineering and a delight to walk. The views west from this part of the walk take in some of the wildest, most rugged and least visited parts of the Black Mountain, where again ancient cairns crown the summits.

With the differing rocks underlying the plant life, you naturally get a variety of wild flowers. A favourite, in season, is the sweet-tasting but purple-staining bilberry. If you follow this walk in bilberry season, allow plenty of extra time for berry picking/eating and take a tub to carry home the fruit for pie making!

The skies are home to a variety of birds, most notable being buzzards, ravens and, if you are lucky, the comparatively rare and very beautiful red kite. Semi-wild ponies grace the hills and their foals look very sweet as they gambol among the watchful adult ponies.

Enjoy this walk in fine weather (and be careful on the rocky sections) for some of the finest walking and best views in Carmarthenshire.

The Route

From the car park, cross the road to the open land opposite, turn left and continue, roughly parallel to the road, past and through old sand quarries as well as by shake holes, for approximately one and a quarter miles.

1. Once you are past the access track to Cwar Penrhiw-wen, an old sand quarry, on the opposite side of the road, you start descending slightly, following sheep tracks, faint quarry tracks and the open hill for approximately three-quarters of a mile. Cross a well-defined quarry track and the often dry stream bed of Nant Gaws as you go. The first half of this section takes you through small, old quarries, the second half across open hillside. Stay roughly parallel to the road, without climbing over much, and approximately 50 metres away from it. You will be surprised at how little the road and traffic are noticed.

2. Once you have covered approximately three-quarters of a mile, you drop down on to a faint, but recognisable, slightly embanked quarry track which almost delineates the changeover from lime-

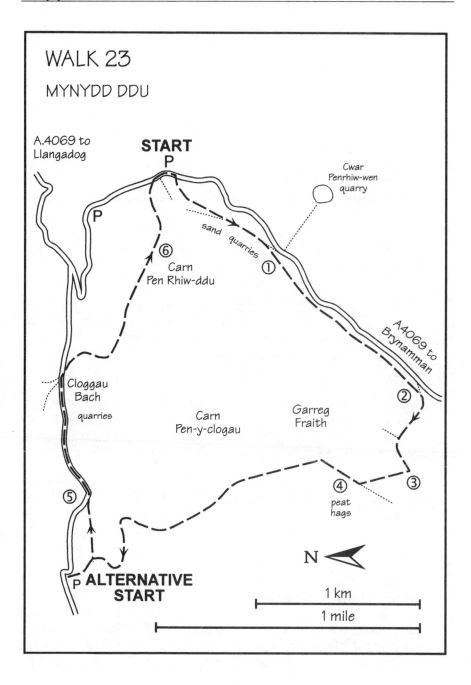

WALK 23
MYNYDD DDU

A.4069 to
Llangadog

START
P

Cwar
Penrhiw-wen
quarry

P

sand quarries

①

⑥
Carn
Pen Rhiw-ddu

A4069 to
Brynamman

Cloggau
Bach

②

quarries

Carn
Pen-y-clogau

Garreg
Fraith

⑤

④

③

peat
hags

P ALTERNATIVE
START

N

1 km

1 mile

stone crags to the flatter, boggier millstone grit terrain. Turn right and follow the track, bearing left at an obvious fork, then on, under and through small quarries, until it peters out in an almost circular, shallow quarry.

3. From here head just west of north, following sheep trods over the open hill. After about 325 metres you should come across the old 'Roman road', which here runs diagonally left to right. Fairly obvious with its levelled surface and stone 'kerbs', the track lies between the quarries and some peat hags. If you get muddy feet you have probably missed it while admiring the stunning views west.

4. Turn right on to the track and follow it roughly north-east. Soon it clips the edge of the boggy area and loses definition, then swings left, climbs out of the dip and regains its obvious kerbs and levelled surface as it crosses the flank of the hill.

The track is followed for approximately one and a quarter miles, giving superb views until, after descending wide zigzags down towards Brest Cwm Llwyd, you come to an obvious fork. Turn right down to the road at a charming spot where a bridge crosses the stream.

5. Turn right and follow the road for about 800 metres to where a marshy track enters the old quarries on your right at Clogau Bach. Follow this track into the quarries, initially almost parallel to the quiet road, past old quarry faces and ruined limekilns.

Once the hairpin bend of the main road comes into view, go more south-east and upwards through a maze of gullies, tracks and trods out of the quarries and across the open hill, heading for the skyline 'pimple' of Carn Pen Rhiw Ddu, which stands out quite clearly.

6. The closer you get to this probably Bronze Age cairn, the less you can see of it, and as you breast the last rocky rampart and stumble up to it, you realise just how small, yet well-sited, it is. From the cairn you can look down on the start, roughly east-south-east of this point. A simple stroll down the hillside, skirting the largest of the sand quarries to the left, soon has you back to your car.

24: Carmarthen

Distance: 9 miles (14.5 km)

Time: 5 to 6 hours

Maps: OS Pathfinders 1058 Llanboidy and Cynwyl Elfed, 1081 St Clears and Laugharne, 1082 Cross Hands and Pontyberem and 1059 Carmarthen. OS Landranger 159 Swansea and Gower.

Start: St Peter's Church 415 202

Terrain: A wide mix of green lanes, field paths, suburbia and rural lanes. Muddy in places.

Nearest Town: Carmarthen(!)

Parking: Ample car parks in town. Note that nearest car park has four hours maximum stay.

Refreshments: Everything you need in Carmarthen. None outside.

Stiles: 5

Suitable for: All. Dogs on leads in farmland, please.

Along the way

Carmarthen is once again in the position of being the county seat of the old County of Carmarthenshire now that Dyfed has been broken up to recreate the counties of Pembrokeshire, Carmarthenshire and Ceredigion.

On a site of great historical importance, Carmarthen has been settled since the Iron Age with a large hill fort at nearby Merlin's Hill. In the year AD75 the Romans constructed a fort, probably in the area around King Street and Spilman Street, and this was the first stage in the development of the important port town of Moridunum. The town had a thriving port using the tidal Towy estuary to reach the sea, and its name came from the Celtic Mor (sea) and Dinas (fort) -

hence Moridunum which comes down to us now as Caer-Mori-Dunum. Carmarthen, the sea fort.

The important, self-governing Roman city, or civitas, one of only two in Wales, can still have its typical 'playing card' shape traced in the street patterns in the eastern side of the town. Few other remains can now be traced, though a substantial town house with underfloor heating was excavated during the construction of the St Peter Street car park, and the impressive remains of a 5000 seat amphitheatre can be visited at the eastern end of Priory Street. This is one of only seven such amphitheatres surviving in Britain and is well worth a detour from the walk.

With the decline of Rome in the fifth century, Carmarthen slid into obscurity and the Dark Ages. During this time a small Christian, perhaps Irish, community settled in Carmarthen, probably using an old Roman cemetery area to the east of the Roman town. Little is known of the area until the Norman era, though legend has it that Carmarthen was the home of Merlin, King Arthur's wizard, confidant and friend. The Normans built two castles in Carmarthen, the first being one and a half miles downstream of the town, then a more enduring one on the land by Nott Square. For a while there were two towns called Carmarthen, each based around a castle, a situation which lasted until the reign of Henry VIII.

The Normans subdued the Celtic Christian church and Carmarthen church was given to the Benedictine monks and then Augustinian Canons. However, Welsh influence remained and the famous *Black Book of Carmarthen* was written, the oldest book of vernacular Welsh poetry, now housed in the National Library of Wales, Aberystwyth.

By the 13th century, the town was the financial, administrative and judicial centre for South Wales, as Edward 1 set out to conquer North Wales. The town grew fast with the castle being rebuilt, the town enclosed by strong walls and churches founded. By 1260 it had spread beyond the walls and a Franciscan monastery had been founded. Llewellyn the Great sacked the castle in 1215, and in 1405 Owain Glyndwr ravaged the undefended parts of the town and more walls were built to avoid a repetition of the bloodshed.

The town flourished as a market centre as well as a centre of Welsh culture, with the port important in the wool trade. In the 16th century the Mayor was also Admiral of the Port and an Admiralty

River Tywi

Court was set up. In addition, a Customs House was built to deal with the important foreign and coastal sea trade. By the 18th century, Carmarthen was the largest and most important port in Wales.

The religious reformation during the 16th century saw Bishop Ferrar perish at the stake in front of the castle, while the first Welsh New Testament was written just outside Carmarthen. The castle which surrendered twice to Owain Glyndwr, was also fought over in the English Civil War and was destroyed in 1660, though parts were later used as a gaol. All that now remain are parts of the keep, curtain wall and gatehouse. The County offices now hold most of the castle site.

The Methodist revival of the 18th century saw schools established along with a range of chapels, and Carmarthen also became a printing centre with perhaps nine printers working in the town.

Surprisingly, Carmarthen has been the seat of heavy industry as well as a market town, with rolling mills, furnaces and tin mills being established in the 1700s, and surviving booms and busts until the 19th century. Still growing, and an important market town and shopping centre, Carmarthen is the gateway to West Wales. However, the town does not forget its history and traditions, with coracle fishing still carried out on the Towy, using craft subtly different to those used on any other river. The coracle actually forms part of the town's coat of arms.

A visit to the Carmarthen Museum in nearby Abergwili (open 10.00 to 16.30, Monday to Saturday) is recommended, as are explorations of the town, wandering through the market and ancient streets at random to get to know the town intimately.

Along this walk you will pass many beautiful gardens, while, along with a great variety of native wild flowers, you will also pass through areas of more exotic plants such as palm trees and semi-wild pampas grass. The wild life is quite varied and the birdlife includes buzzards and other birds of prey as well as more common species of wood and meadow land birds.

The Route

The walk starts from St Peter's Church, which dates from 1100 and contains many points of interest including some superb stained glass (ancient and modern) and a pagan Roman altar, making it worth a prolonged visit in its own right. The route then takes you past a bus stop, with ceramic tiles illustrating the history of Carmarthen, and across the main road and south-east down Parade Road and down left on to the Parade.

This road and its continuation, the Esplanade, were built in 1798 as town houses for the country gentry, and give superb views over the Towy Valley. Many of the buildings are architecturally interesting. You also pass the old Presbyterian College (1840-1963) which is a continuation of the Bryllywarch Academy founded in 1672 or earlier. An indication of the mild Carmarthen climate is the sight of palm trees along this part of the walk. As well as the river, the valley holds the remains of the old railway line which is now mainly used as a walking route, its industrial days now passed.

At the end of the Esplanade continue past the dead end sign and the old Grammar School, now private dwellings, and along Priory Row. Where the road turns sharp left some 150 metres from the end of the Esplanade, go straight on along the footpath alongside the old railway line. The 'wild' flowers along this section include lilac and Himalayan balsam. Approaching the fenced builders' merchant's yard, the path becomes surfaced. Follow this path as it skirts the builders' yard, then swings left, zigzags and climbs up to the main road opposite a petrol station.

1. Cross the road with care as it is fast and busy, and either go straight up Reservoir Road opposite or first divert left for some 400 metres up to the Roman amphitheatre. Reservoir Road is a quiet lane that leads you up to a car park by Cwm Oernant Reservoirs.

2. Built in a very pleasant valley, the reservoirs have been developed by the council as a recreational facility, with a maze of footpaths in the wooded areas around the two reservoirs. These are home to a variety of bird and plant life including reeds, water lilies, moorhens etc. A wander around this almost deserted and beautiful spot is recommended as an addition to the walk.

   From the car park a footpath runs up in front of the Lake View and up between fields to the quiet, rural hamlet of Cwm Oernant. Turn left when you reach the lane, Springfield Lane, and follow this for about 300 metres to where the lane swings right.

3. On your left, slate steps lead up to an iron kissing gate. Go through a second kissing gate by an electricity pole and take the path down St John the Baptist Hill. This takes you down an ancient route behind some houses to Capel Evan Road. Continue straight on down this suburban road for about 200 metres to a crossroads, with Park Hall on your left and Longacre Road on your right. Turn right up this one-way street that curves around the back of the school and follow it to a T-junction with the lower end of Springfield Road.

   Bear left on Wellfield Road to a staggered crossroads with Waterloo Terrace, Brewery Road and Pentrefelin Road. Cross over and follow Pentrefelin Road as it winds past a tyre services and through a housing estate to a major T-junction with Fountain Hall Terrace. Turn left, then first right by a petrol station to follow Glannant Road and College Road for approximately 400 metres to an iron kissing gate by the entrance to Glannant Flats.

4. Through the kissing gate, a narrow footpath winds up to the end of a cul-de-sac. At the entrance to the cul-de-sac, cross the road to another kissing gate by the side of a house. This leads you into a narrow, deeply-hedged path and through some pampas grass to yet another kissing gate into a field. Follow the right-hand boundary around one-and-a-half sides of the field to a rusted solid kissing gate, then diagonally left across the next field, heading in the direction of farm buildings in the middle distance. This leads you to a kissing gate.

Go through this and turn right to follow the right-hand boundary under the bank, then through a gate. Follow the bank across the next field to reach the far boundary by electricity poles. Turn left and follow the boundary into a green lane. Follow this for approximately 150 metres, crossing a stream and continuing between a hedge and a stream to steps up to the road by Rhyd y Bont Farm.

5. Turn left and follow the road for 200 metres to a point just after the road crosses a stream. Here a track joins from the left and there is a post box set in the wall. Turn left up the track and go straight on through a gate ahead beyond the houses.

The right of way follows the left-hand boundary until just beyond a brick-built building (pumping station?), where the path drops left through two kissing gates to follow the right-hand boundary of the lower field. This leads through another kissing gate and along the hedge to a track leading to Tre-Fechan-Fach Farm. The kissing gates beyond the brick building are somewhat overgrown and obstructed. However, if they are too overgrown to use, by staying above the hedge line, you can reach the same track to the farmyard by going through a series of gates.

6. Go through the farmyard – beware of the dog – and follow the farm drive, bearing left at the fork. Continue along a lane to a crossroads by Trinity College. Turn right up Pentremeurig Road and follow this as it turns into a country lane and drops down to a bridge over Tawelan Brook.

7. Just beyond the bridge, go left up a track to Dawelan. The 'Beware of the Dog' sign is intimidating, but I have always found the dogs to

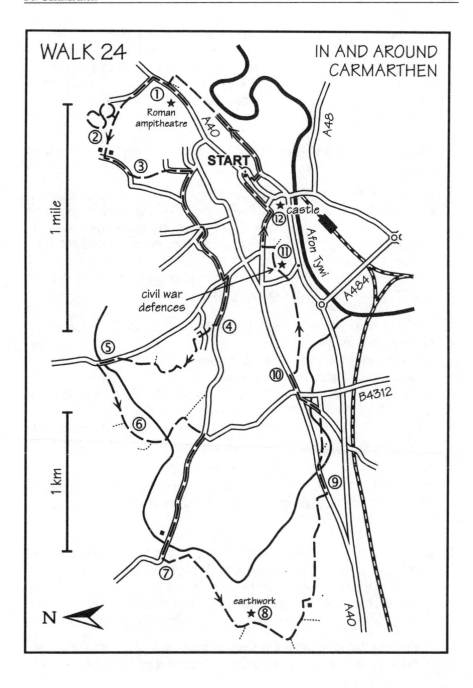

WALK 24

IN AND AROUND
CARMARTHEN

Roman
ampitheatre

START

castle

Afon Tywi

civil war
defences

1 mile

1 km

earthwork

N

be chained up by the house, well away from the path. Where the main tracks go left to sheds and right to the house, go straight on up a green lane into the woods. The continuation of this lane runs on from the woods and up to Trebersed Farm and gives excellent views. On reaching the farmyard, turn left across the front of the farmhouse and down the farm lane.

8. Note the remains of an ancient earthwork between the lane and the copse to your left.

   At the bottom of the slope turn left on to a lane which you follow for about 200 metres, to where it takes a right-angled turn to the right by some old farm buildings. Instead of following the lane, go straight on along a green lane ahead which goes beyond modern factory-type buildings. Keep to this ancient route as it winds its often muddy way between high hedges for approximately three-quarters of a mile down to the road at Johnstown.

9. Turn left on reaching the road, then after about 200 metres cross and take the footpath that leaves a lay-by and cross the stream by a wooden footbridge. Cross a driveway and follow the footpath through a kissing gate and between houses to the end of a cul-de-sac. The old footpath now seems to have been buried by the bungalows, so follow the road to the T-junction at the bottom, where you turn left and recross the stream by a pedestrian bridge parallel to the old stone bridge.

   At the next T-junction, turn right and go straight over the crossroads by the Friends Arms pub and up the hill towards the obelisk of the Picton Monument, raised in memory of General Picton of Waterloo fame.

10. Some 150 metres up the hill from the crossroads, turn right into the dead end road of Maes y Derwen. Between numbers 9 and 11 a sign up to the left, 'llwybr cyhoeddus', points you up a footpath that leads across a field dominated by the Picton Monument, and through a set of allotments on a good track to the rugby pitches.

    Follow the left hedge by the pitches and through the car park beyond to meet the road opposite MFI. Turn left up to the main road, which you cross to take the footpath signed to the police station and town centre.

11. This path takes you through some very visible remains of English Civil War town defences and by a detailed interpretation board telling the story of these earthworks. Go on along the side of Tesco to a car park. Turn left through the car park to Lammas Street, where you turn right by the Tourist Information Centre and continue down to Guildhall Square with its memorial to the dead of the Boer War. Take the lane to the right of the Guildhall (built 1767) and up St Mary's Street, once the main route up to the castle.

12. On entering Nott Square, the few remains of the castle are visible ahead. Turn left and cross Nott Square, then follow King Street back up to the start of the walk at the far end of this shopping street.

Around Carmarthen

Carmarthen has an interesting history and a wander around its streets will be worthwhile for anyone with energy to spare after this walk. Visits to the churches, especially St Peter's, and the historic market are worth the effort, while the lanes around Nott Square, the old part of the town, will reveal mediaeval and Georgian architecture.

An in-depth exploration of the history, culture and architecture of Carmarthen and its surroundings would take weeks, and cover more miles than this short taster can cover. Carmarthen has hidden jewels well worth discovering by further reading and walking.

25: Pumsaint

Distance: main walk – 5 miles (8km), with the mine walk – 6 miles (10km), shortest option – 3 miles (5km). Alternative start – add 1mile (1.5km).

Time: Between 2 hours (short option) and 4 hours (longest option)

Maps: OS Pathfinder 1013 Cilycwm and Pumsaint, OS Landranger 146 Lampeter, Llandovery and Surrounding Area.

Start: Dolaucothi Gold Mines Car Park 662 403. Gates locked when gold mines closed. Gold mines open 10.00 to 18.00 in summer and 10.00 to 17.00 out of season. Alternative Start: Free car park with 24 hour access at Visitor Centre in Pumsaint village 656 405. Please use this start if you intend being early or late on the walk.

Nearest Towns: Lampeter and Llandovery

Terrain: Good paths, tracks (muddy in places), lanes and one section (by permission) across private land.

Parking: See Start

Refreshments: Tea rooms (excellent) at gold mine, Dolaucothi Arms Hotel, Pumsaint.

Stiles: 12

Suitable for: All. Dogs on leads at all time in farmland, please.

Along the way

Pumsaint is a small hamlet with a fascinating history and some interesting legends. The name of the hamlet is said to originate from five saints (pump meaning five) who lived in the area – semi-mythical, Dark Age, Celtic Christian characters named Gwyno, Gwynnore, Gwyn, Celymin and Ceitho.

A stone set on a mound near the start of the walk is known as the 'Five Saints' Stone', or Carreg Pumsaint, and is where the five are said to have huddled to shelter from a storm, leaving indentations of their heads and backs on four sides of the rock. Where the fifth sheltered is open to question, and with marks on four sides, some of the saints must have had poor shelter! Legend also casts doubt on the saintliness of the five as the devil is said to have caught them napping and imprisoned them in the lower levels of the adjacent gold mines. An inquisitive local girl called Gwen wanted to see the captive saints and the devil led her down to visit them. However, the saints, on awaking, took her captive (purpose unspecified) and kept her in the mine, only allowing her out when a storm was blowing. Perhaps she, too, sheltered by the rock!

Less romantically, the Saints' Stone is probably an anvil rock from a machine designed to crush the gold-bearing rock.

Open from May to September, the gold mines themselves are looked after by the National Trust and were worked from Celtic times until their final closure as a commercial undertaking in 1938. A superb underground tour – complete with horrific ghost story – is available. Above ground there are also excellent displays of 1930s mining machinery, a guided tour, shop, video display, toilets and a tea room serving excellent cakes and bacon butties among other light meals. Once you have paid to enter the site (no charge if only visiting the tea shop), there is a further one hour stroll available on the Miners' Way, a leafleted walk around the mines which is well worth following.

There is some discrepancy about who actually worked the mines: some say it was slaves who lived in appalling conditions, while eminent historians contend that it was local Celtic people – who would also have lived in appalling conditions! The Roman soldiers overseeing the slaves/locals were based in a fort at Pumsaint, the barrack block of which, dating back to approximately the first century AD was excavated fairly recently. Part of the seven-mile leat built by the Romans (or at least their slaves/local workers) to supply water to the mines can be seen and is a protected Ancient Monument.

The surrounding hills are dotted with remains of Bronze Age and later cairns, standing stones and earthworks, an indication of how long man has enjoyed this area. More recent historic remains to be seen in the area include a tree-covered mound by the Five Saints' Stone, which could be a Norman castle mound (or a spoil heap from the mines) and the remains of Dolaucothi Mansion. This was a home

Dolaucothi gold mines

of the Lloyd Johnes family, owners of the Dolaucothi Estate, until it was bequeathed to the National Trust in the 1950s. Although the mansion was demolished in 1955, the remaining features include the stables and coach house, now converted into a base camp for National Trust volunteer workers, the wall of the walled garden, and the Dolaucothi farmhouse.

George Borrow visited the area on his walk through wild Wales when writing his famous book, which was first published in 1862 and is still in print. He found the inn to be good and comfortable with clean beds – a rare luxury in those days. Although he never visited Dolaucothi Mansion, he walked down the avenue of 'very noble oaks' and thought he 'had never seen a more pleasing locality'. He describes the mansion as 'a plain but comfortable gentleman's seat with wings' and thought it would be a very satisfactory place to live – given a decent income.

On the walk you will also see coppiced woodland at Allt Dinbeth, part of which is a SSSI, and Cefncoedmawr Farm, a collection of attractive 18th-century buildings.

With its wooded paths and riverside walking, this route uses footpaths maintained by the National Trust across their estate and Forestry Commission tracks, and offers superb views of this historic valley. The wildlife is rich and varied with numerous wild flowers and a good selection of bird species to be seen, including the beautiful red kite. More paths are being created over the Dolaucothi Estate by the National Trust, so in future there will be even more choice of walks in this lovely valley.

I would like to thank Mr Huw Davies of Llandre Farm, Pumsaint, for permission to cross his land and use his bridge on this walk. The use of this section of the walk is strictly at your own risk and all dogs must be kept under strict control when crossing Mr Davies' land to avoid disturbing livestock. If you find this unacceptable, please follow the short alternative route and thereby by-pass this section of the walk. My thanks also to staff of the National Trust for their help in researching this walk.

The Route

The Main Route

From the gold mine's car park, take the path that heads away from the road and swings right above the River Cothi, leading you through a picnic site to an attractive bridge.

1. Cross the bridge, go through the gate ahead and cross the parkland of the Dolaucothi Estate to a wooden bridge – stile – board-walk opposite. The farm buildings can be seen off to your right. Cross the bridge – stile – board-walk, noting the strange sight of a tree growing out of or over what seems to be the arch of a spring house on your right. Climb the steps up to the track above. Turn left on the track to join the farm drive, which leads you up to a major track junction.

2. This is where the route from Pumsaint Visitor Centre joins the main walk.

   Opposite the drive down to the farm there are a pair of field gates, and to their right a pedestrian gate. Go through the pedestrian gate and cross the field diagonally, heading almost due north on the faint remains of a levelled track.

3. This leads you up to a stile in a sharp corner. Cross this to reach the right-hand of two pedestrian gates. It leads on to a clear path up through woodland which follows a charming stream with views to the right over the valley.

4. At the top of the woods, the track exits over a stile into a field. A faint path circles right along the line of an old bank and hedge and across the top of a boggy area to a metal gate. Go through the gate and turn sharp left uphill, following the left-hand boundary up to an OS trig point.

5. Here you are rewarded by superb views all around – over the Cothi Valley and up into Mid Wales. It is a good place for a break before you continue along the fence and over a stile in the corner into more woodland.

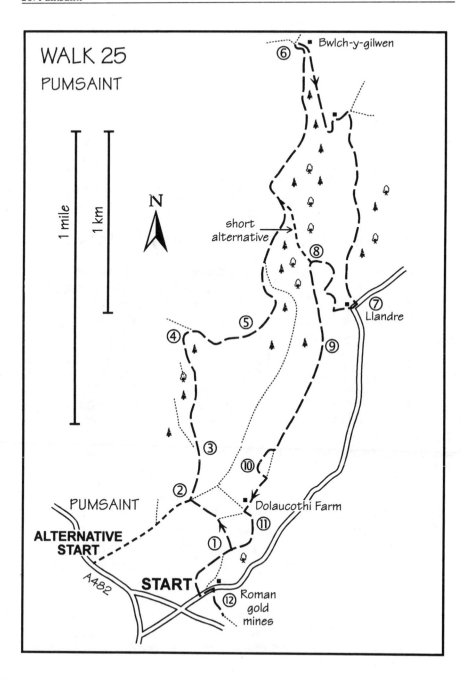

WALK 25
PUMSAINT

1 mile

1 km

N

Bwlch-y-gilwen

short
alternative

Llandre

PUMSAINT

ALTERNATIVE
START

A482

START

Dolaucothi Farm

Roman
gold
mines

A faint path hugs the left boundary of the forestry and eventually leads you down to a good track that runs northwards along the top of the plantations. Many fine oaks and other broadleaf trees have been left on the fringe of the conifers, making it a more pleasant prospect than most forestry walks, while good views are afforded from many spots.

For the long option of this walk, you follow this track for approximately three-quarters of a mile to where it passes through a gate and joins a lane at Bwlch-y-Gilwen.

A short option – which avoids the private land at Llandre – leaves the track after some 400 metres, dropping right down a forestry track to rejoin the main route near the bridge at Llandre, point 8.

6. From Bwlch-y-Gilwen the walk turns right on the lane, which is followed down to and across a bridge over a tributary of the Cothi, and up to a T-junction with another quiet lane. Turn right down to a bridge over the Cothi and on, under Allt Dinbeth Hill, to a T-junction with the quiet Cwrt-y-Cadno to Pumsaint road.

7. Turn right at the junction and almost immediately leave the road through the entrance to Llandre Farm (note the letter box built into the wall to the left of the gate). A public right of way leads between the house on your right and farm buildings on your left to a gate opposite. Going through this puts you on a muddy track down along the left-hand hedge of the field ahead and down to a ford across the Cothi. This is impractical to use except in severe droughts.

The land owner, Mr Davies, has given permission for walkers using this guide to follow the river bank right up to his bridge across the river **at their own risk**, providing dogs are kept on leads and under control. Please respect Mr Davies' land and livestock and do nothing to cause him to reconsider his decision to allow access to this section of the walk.

8. Once across the bridge, follow the track up to the gate in the forestry ahead and through this to rejoin the short alternative walk some 60 metres into the woods.

Just before the track bends sharp right, a faint waymarked path on the left leaves the track and follows the river below southwards, eventually joining the old track to the now unusable ford.

9. The obvious path continues roughly south-south-west as a tree-lined green lane, following the top of a steep bank above the flood plain of the river. It continues as a field path along the left-hand side of a couple of fields. It is from along this part that you can make out the remains of the Roman aqueduct on the hills opposite.

10. Just as Dolaucothi Farm comes into view at a field gate, the path drops left with the hedge on your right, down to a stile at the foot of the slope. Turn right over the stile and follow the right-hand field boundary round to a stile into the yard of Dolaucothi Farm. Note the bell tower on the farmhouse.

11. Turn left on to the track alongside the wall of the old mansion's walled garden, and follow the track round to the bridge met early in the walk. Retrace your steps back to the road at the car park of the gold mine and turn left, following the road some 100 metres to find Carreg Pumsaint in a grassy area opposite Ogofau Cottage.

12. A path in the right-hand corner behind the stone leads up to the gold mines and you can (and I recommend you do) extend the walk by following The Miners' Way, a leafleted walk from the mines through Roman and later workings. There is an admission charge for visiting the mines and this walk, but it is well worth the cost.

If you have the time, an extended visit including the underground tour and panning for gold is definitely recommended and makes this walk a memorable day out.

Alternative Start

From the Visitor Centre car park, turn left on the main road, then left again after 50 metres, up the wooded track to Cefn Coed Mawr and Dolaucothi Farms. Join the main route at point 2.

After visiting the mines, follow the start of the main route back to this point and retrace your footsteps along the track to Pumsaint village.

A Welsh Language Primer

Visitors may be surprised to find Welsh being spoken as a first language in this area, while place names may at first prove unpronounceable. This section will help you to understand and pronounce Welsh words and phrases. Firstly, this is how the less-familiar letters are pronounced:

a	=	ah
c	=	k (hard)
ch	=	as in the Scottish 'loch'
dd	=	th in 'the'
e	=	eh
f	=	v
ff	=	f
g	=	as in 'go' (hard)
i	=	ee
ll	=	almost a 'th' sound. Say 'l' and gently blow through the tongue in this position
o	=	oh
th	=	as in 'through'
w	=	often as 'oo'. Cwm (valley); sounds like 'coomb'
y	=	as e in 'the' (y or yr), or as i. Dyffryn therefore sounds like 'duffrin'.

Words used in place names

Here is a small selection of Welsh words that are often seen on OS maps either in isolation or as parts of place names:

aber	=	estuary, river-mouth or confluence of streams
afon	=	river
bach, fach	=	small
bedd	=	grave
betws	=	chapel or oratory
blaen	=	head of the valley
bont, pont	=	bridge
braich	=	arm
brith	=	speckled
bryn	=	hill
bwlch	=	pass, defile
bychan	=	little
cadair	=	chair
cae	=	field

caer	=	fort
capel	=	chapel
carn, carnedd	=	pile of stones
carreg	=	rock
castell	=	castle
cefn	=	ridge
celli, gelli	=	grove
clogwyn	=	precipice
coch	=	red
coed	=	woodland
cors, gors	=	bog
craig	=	rock
crib	=	narrow ridge
croes	=	cross
cwm	=	valley
dinas	=	fort
dol, ddol	=	meadow
drws	=	door
dwr	=	water
dyffryn	=	valley
eglwys	=	church
esgair	=	mountain shoulder
fawr, mawr	=	big
felin, melin	=	mill
ffordd	=	road
ffynnon	=	well, spring
foel, moel	=	rounded hill
fynydd, mynydd	=	mountain
gam	=	crooked
glan	=	bank, shore
glas, las	=	blue, green
glyder	=	head
glyn	=	glen
gwastad	=	plain, level ground
gwern	=	marsh
gwyn	=	white
gwynt	=	wind
hafod	=	summer dwelling
hen	=	old
hendre	=	winter dwelling
hir	=	long
isa, isaf	=	lower
llan	=	sacred enclosure, church
llethr	=	slope
llwyd	=	grey
llwyn	=	grove
llyn	=	lake
maen	=	stone

maes	=	field
morfa	=	coastal marsh
nant	=	brook, stream
newydd	=	new
ogof	=	cave
oleu	=	light
pant, bant	=	small hollow
pen	=	head, top
penrhyn	=	promontory
pentre, pentref	=	village
pistyll	=	spout, cataract
plas	=	mansion
pwll	=	pool
rhaeadr	=	waterfall
rhiw	=	hill
rhos	=	moorland, marsh
rhyd	=	ford
sarn	=	paved way, causeway
sych	=	dry
tan	=	under
tarren	=	hill
tir	=	land
traeth	=	stretch of shore
tre	=	town, hamlet
tri	=	three
trwyn	=	nose, promontory
twll	=	hole
ty	=	house
tyddyn	=	smallholding
ucha, uchaf	=	upper
waun	=	moor
y	=	the, of the
yn	=	in
ynys	=	island
ysgol	=	school, ladder
ystrad	=	valley floor, strath

Useful and polite phrases to learn are:

Bore da (bor-eh-da)	=	good morning
Diolch (dee-olch)	=	thank you
Dim diolch	=	no thank you

Watch out for contractions of some words. For example the name of the hill 'Foel Drygarn' can also be rendered as 'Foeldrygarn'. Also some Welsh words (for example, place names) are said to 'mutate' – in that their spellings may change depending on usage, particularly in place names. For example, Pont (bridge) changes (mutates) to 'bont' in Pen y Bont and Mair (Mary) becomes Fair in 'Llanfair'.

HERITAGE WALKS IN PEMBROKESHIRE

John Fenna

Discover the pleasures of Pembrokeshire away from tourist honeypots "an ideal introduction to the rich natural, historic, industrial and legendary heritage of this land of contrasts." Wales Tourist Board TRAVEL NEWS. *(£6.95)*

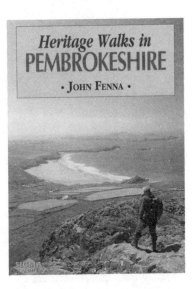

WALKS IN MYSTERIOUS WALES

Laurence Main

Follow the spirit paths of Wales - visit the most sacred and secret sites and discover ancient traditions of this historic country in the company of a leading expert. And, while you're discovering Welsh heritage, enjoy some excellent walks across the length and breadth of this ancient land. *(£6.95)*

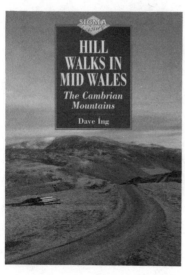

HILL WALKS IN MID WALES
The Cambrian Mountains

Dave Ing

This is one of the very few books to explore the pleasures of walking in Mid Wales - far from the big mountains of Snowdonia and away from the crowds, yet so accessible for a day in the hills. (£7.95)